Selection and Matching Turbocharger to Large Propulsion Engine Performance

Hamid Keshavarzi (Ch. Eng)

Liverpool John Moors University

Book's Name:	Selection and Matching Turbocharger to Large Propulsion Engine Performance
Author:	**Keshavarzi, Hamid, 1957 -**
ISBN:	978-600-97773-6-5
Editor:	Abedian, Morvarid, 1997 -
Publisher:	Degarandishan Publishing House
Specifications:	140 pages
Dewey Decimal Classification:	621/436
NLAI Registry Number:	4901655
Edited By:	Morvarid Abedian Kasgari

ACKNOWLEDGEMENT

Table of Contents

Chapter 3

Turbocharger matching

List of figures

x

List of tables

Abstract

The *diesel engine* is a compression-ignition internal combustion heat engine which can be operated in both the four- and two-stroke cycle. This high efficiency translates to good fuel economy and low greenhouse gas emissions.

Pressure charging is the process of force-feeding air into the combustion chamber of the diesel engine. All marine propulsion diesel engines have an air-charge system with an exhaust driven turbine. This is referred to as turbocharging. A modern *turbocharger* has simple, modular design, aimed at improving overall life cycle. Developments in *turbocharger's* component design and manufacture all contribute to this goal. The key design criteria include:

- High specific flow rates
- High efficiencies and reliability
- Low noise emissions
- Ease of maintenance and mounting
- Long-service life

When comparing similar rated engines, in terms of *environmental protection*, one fitted with a modern turbocharger will consume some 10-15% less fuel while reducing gaseous emissions by equally significant amounts. However it is not just in fuel efficiency where *environmental protection* benefits lie, in noise and vibration for example, modern turbocharger has succeeded in lowering noise emissions to less than $105 dB(A)$ at one meter distance and has improved vibration characteristics, by having kept the natural frequencies well above any exciting frequencies from the diesel engine.

In connection with *turbocharger matching* to marine propulsion diesel engine, years of experience have enabled makers of turbocharger to develop a simple, semi-empirical method for selecting the optimum turbocharger for any propulsion engine, turbocharging system, output data and ambient conditions, at low computation cost and with sufficient accuracy. The calculation of turbocharging system with pulsating admission of the turbine is based on an empirical 'pulse factor' and can thus be reduced to a simple computation of a system with 'equivalent constant-pressure admission' of the turbine. All the empirical characteristic variables are so defined that they can be determined from the usual, available numerical data from acceptance tests and turbocharger adaptation tests, and also by step-by-step computation of real working cycle.

Key words

Marine propulsion diesel engine, Pressure-charging, Turbocharger, Environmental Protection and Turbocharger matching

Acknowledgements

I have in this dissertation work, a distillation of the wisdom and knowledge acquired from continual efforts of successful turbocharger designers.

My special gratitude to Mr. Markos and Mr. E. Meier of ABB Turbo System Ltd, Baden, Switzerland, and Mr. T. Schmitz of MAN B&W Diesel AG, Augsburg, Germany who provided me with a lot of valuable data and useful information about turbocharger technology and matching.

Last but not the least I thank Mr. A. Saajedi who contributed so much to this dissertation work as supervisor as he frequently worked out to a complete, well-balanced text in a process through which he acted as a critical reader, and he indeed gave very valuable suggestions for improvement both technically and educationally.

CHAPTER ONE

Diesel engine

1.1 History

The first decade of the 1900s proved to be a time of experimentation and success in the area of diesel engine design and manufacture. The installation of diesel engines into river and coastal craft was eagerly anticipated, however, there still remained some skepticism in the performance abilities of the combustion engines on long, seafaring journeys. Rudolf Diesel patented his engine in Germany, on 28th of February 1892 and he later obtained patent rights in most industrialized countries. In 1894, Diesel contacted David Halley, the managing director of Burmeister and Wain (B&W), requesting the company experiment with his design, which eventually laid the ground for a most successful career in the design and manufacture of diesel engines.[1]

While the *Selandia*, built 1912, remains heralded as the first seagoing diesel engine vessel, in 1905, the 125 ton vessel, Venoga, built by Sulzer, became the world's first diesel engine vessel and was used on Lake Geneva. [2]

1.2 Working principle

Nearly all motive power is derived from heat using some form of heat engine. A heat engine requires a source of hot energy. We get this by burning fossil fuel or by nuclear fusion. [3]

The diesel engine is a compression-ignition internal combustion heat engine which may be operated in both the four-stroke and two-stroke cycle. The intention of this dissertation is to focus only on marine large two-stroke diesel propulsion engines. The combustion process can be theoretically modeled by applying thermodynamic laws of mass and energy conservation to the processes in the engine cylinder. Basic design and performance parameters in diesel engines include compression ratio, swept volume, clearance volume, a number of scavenging characteristics in two-stroke engines, power output, indicated power, mechanical efficiency, indicated and brake mean effective pressures, specific fuel consumption, and etc. [4]

All internal combustion diesel engine, require air to produce power. The air is ingested and combined with fuel before being compressed in the combustion chamber and then burned to generate power. Of the two ingredients needed to produce this power, air is generally the more difficult to deliver to the combustion chamber. This is primarily due to the fact that a naturally aspirated engine must "inhale" the air using the vacuum generated when a piston traveling downward on its intake stroke creates a low-pressure environment in the intake tract. How effectively this process is able to fill the cylinders is a major factor in determining how much power the engine is capable of developing, and is measured in terms of volumetric efficiency $\eta_{volumetric}$. An engine capable of completely filling the volume of its cylinders by the end of the intake stroke would have 100 percent volumetric efficiency $\eta_{volumetric}$. There are a number of factors that hinder this efficiency. These include the shape, size, and length of the intake tract, the quality of the piston seal, the timing of the valve events, and the efficiency of the exhaust evacuation during the preceding stroke. The deficit in cylinder fill imposed by these factors (and others) is referred to in terms of pumping losses. A typical naturally aspirating engine operates at around 80 to 85 percent of $\eta_{volumetric}$. However in order to overcome these obstacles, or at least to diminish them, air will have to be forced into the cylinder using external means rather than relying on the   draw   of   the   descending   piston.

1.3 Class and construction

There are two classes of diesel engines: two-stroke and four-stroke. Many larger propulsion diesel engines operate on two-stroke cycle. Smaller engines generally use the four-stroke cycle.

With regard to construction, two different types of diesel engines can be distinguished: crosshead engines and trunk piston engines. The engines are built as in-line engines i.e. all cylinders are positioned on one line. Trunk piston engines are also built with two lines of cylinders in a V-configuration, i.e. V-engines. [4]

1.4 Operating modes

In diesel engines, fuel is injected into the engine cylinder near the end of the compression stroke. During a phase known as ignition delay, the fuel spray atomizes into small droplets, vaporizes, and mixes with air. As the piston continues to move closer to top dead center, the mixture temperature reaches the fuel's ignition point, causing instantaneous ignition of some pre-mixed quantity of fuel and air. The balance of fuel that had not participated in premixed combustion is consumed in the rate-controlled combustion phase, also known as diffusion combustion.

The chemical energy stored in the fuels is transformed into mechanical energy at the output shaft in two steps: first, chemical energy is converted into thermal energy by means of a combustion reaction of the fuel, with the air as working medium and; second, the thermal energy is converted into mechanical energy.

The basic diesel cycle consist of air inlet, compression, combustion and expansion, and exhaust. These processes can be achieved in two strokes of the piston or in four strokes, i.e. in a two-stroke cycle or in a four-stroke cycle. [4]

1.5 Cylinder geometry

A stroke is defined as the distance travelled by the piston between the extreme top position and the extreme bottom position: top dead centre (TDC) and bottom dead centre (BDC). The inside diameter of the bore is $D_B[m]$. The stroke-bore ratio λ_s is the ratio of stroke length $L_s[m]$ to bore diameter. The cylinder volume that corresponds with the stroke is the swept volume $V_s[m^3]$, and equals the product of bore area and stroke length. The volume above the piston at BDC is the maximum cylinder volume V_{BDC}, where as the volume above piston at TDC is the clearance or compression volume V_{TDC}. The ratio of V_{BDC} over V_{TDC} is called the geometric compression ratio ε. [4]

$$\lambda = \frac{L_S}{D_B} \text{ (1.1)}$$

$$V_S = A_B.L_S = \frac{\pi}{4}.D_B^2.L_S \text{ (1.2)}$$

1.6 Performance

The efficiency of a diesel engine is much better than the efficiency of a steam plant or a gas turbine; this is true at design load and even more so at part load. The fundamental cause for the high efficiency of a diesel engine is the intermittent character of the combustion, which allows high peak temperatures in the cylinder without causing an extreme continuous thermal loading of the surrounding materials.

As for any other machine involved in energy conversion, the power-speed characteristics, the power density and fuel economy are important issues for marine diesel engine. Other characteristics are maximum obtainable power, air consumption, emissions and costs. [4]

Performance of a marine propulsion diesel engine, broadly speaking, is divided into two categories based on engine speed: low-speed and medium-speed. However medium speed diesel engines have some other application such as electric generation plant prime mover, engines to drive smaller boats and crafts and etc.

Since, not all energy entering the diesel process in the form of fuel is converted into indicated work because of the losses and related efficiencies which are encountered during conversion process of fuel energy to work output the overall, or effective efficiency of an engine is work output divided by heat input.

$$\eta_e = \frac{W_e}{Q_f} \quad (1.3)$$

And in analogy, the indicated efficiency can be defined as the ratio of indicated work and heat input

$$\eta_i = \frac{W_i}{Q_f} \quad (1.4)$$

The diesel engine is still the most frequently used prime mover in merchant marine and its advantages over other prime movers, are that the diesel engine;

- Is the most energy efficient prime mover when compared to gas turbine or steam plant
- Has improved fuel economy with lower greenhouse gas emissions
- Has longer durability, reliability, and fuel safety
- Can handle wide range of fuel quality
- Has high maintainability due to simple technology

The disadvantages of the diesel engine include noise, low specific power output, NO_x and diesel particulate matter emissions, and high cost.

1.7 Power

The power of an engine is generated by the pressure of the working gas on the piston. The mean pressure is expressed as P_{mi} (bar). The friction loss has to be deducted from this, and what remains is the mean effective pressure P_{me} (bar). The power of an engine, P_e in kW, depends on its size and on its speed n_e, and on the mean effective pressure, P_{me} in bars.

$$P_e = \frac{i.V_s.n_e.P_{me}.10^2}{K.60} \, kW \quad (1.5)$$

Where i is the number of cylinder and in general terms, the swept volume is V_s in m^3, the number of revolutions of the crankshaft per complete working cycle is defined by the constant k where;

k =1 for a 2-stroke engine and k =2 for a 4-stroke engine

The effective efficiency of an engine therefore is: $\eta = \frac{P_e}{Q}$ (1.6) where

Q is the energy supplied by fuel.

1.8 Air consumption

Combustion requires oxygen. The oxygen is contained in the combustion air that is trapped in the cylinder. The amount of air required to efficiently burn the fuel is normally related to the amount of fuel; this ratio is called the air-fuel ratio, which is formally defined as:

$$Air - fuel, ratio = \frac{m_{ca}}{m_f} \quad (1.7)$$

By using basic chemistry, the minimum required, so called stoichiometric, amount of air can be determined when the composition of the air is defined and the composition of the fuel is known; this then leads to definition of the stoichiometric air-fuel ratio:

$$\sigma = \frac{m_{ca.min}}{m_f} \quad (1.8)$$

The ratio of the actual amount of combustion air to minimum amount of combustion air is by definition the air excess ratio: $\lambda = \frac{m_{ca}}{m_{ca.min}} \quad (1.9)$

The actual amount of combustion air m_{ca} is bigger than the theoretical $m_{ca.min}$ in order to improve combustion and cool the combustion chamber to maintain temperature within design limits. [4]

1.9 Pressure-charging in marine diesel engine

The goal of pressure charging is to obtain more power from a cylinder of given size, or in other words to increase the power to weight ratio of the diesel engine. In a marine diesel engine which draws its combustion air direct from the atmosphere the density of the induced air charge is approximately the same as the ambient air density. As this air density determines the maximum weight of fuel that can effectively be burned

26

per working stroke in the cylinder, it also determines the maximum power that can be developed by the diesel engine. If, therefore, the charge-air density is increased by the interposition of a suitable compressor between the ambient air and the cylinder, it follows that the weight of air per working stroke is increased and thereby a greater weight of fuel can be burned in the same cylinder, with proportionate augmentation of power.

The power for driving the compressor has an important influence on the operating efficiency of the diesel engine.

For example, it is relatively uneconomical to drive the compressor direct from the engine by chain or other mechanism because some of the additional power is absorbed thereby and there is thus an increase in specific fuel consumption for the extra power obtained. [4]

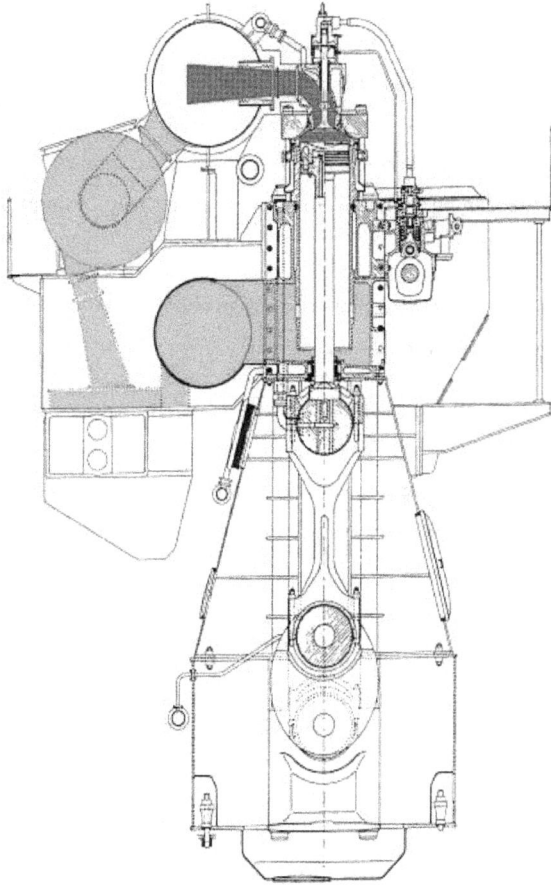

Fig. 1.1: Cut away drawing of a turbo charged diesel engine [5]

In the diesel engine's exhaust gases about 25% of the input energy is available at fairly high temperature. They are therefore a useful, potential source for heat recovery. Usually marine propulsion diesel engines are designed for air intake temperature of up to $45^{o}C$ for tropical conditions and where drawing intake air from the engine room i.e. over $10^{O}C$ higher intake air temperature when intake air is drawn from outside engine room via air ducts. With this increased intake air temperature and the exhaust gases energy available, exhibit enhanced pressure charging via turbocharger (Fig. 1.1).

1.10 Conclusions

The marine diesel engine is today's predominant prime mover used for ship propulsion. The most typical marine propulsion plant of modern merchant ships is a single, slow-speed turbocharged, two-stroke diesel engine directly coupled to the vessel's single, fixed-pitch propeller. This configuration can provide large power outputs (up to 80MW from a single unit) and yet is characterized by operational robustness due to its conceptual simplicity.

The marine diesel engines are reciprocating internal combustion engines. The process of energy conversion in the diesel engine include: air inlet, compression, expansion and exhaust. Combustion normally takes place during expansion.

In all marine propulsion diesel engines, for combustion air and fuel are required. The air is ingested and combined with fuel before being

29

compressed in the combustion chamber and then burned to generate power. Of the two ingredients needed to produce this power, air is generally the more difficult to deliver to the combustion chamber. This is primarily due to the fact that a naturally aspirated engine must "inhale" the air using the vacuum generated when a piston traveling downward on its intake stroke creates a low-pressure environment in the intake tract. A diesel engine capable of completely filling the volume of its cylinders by the end of the intake stroke would have 100 percent volumetric efficiency. With key performance parameters such as mean effective pressure and indicated work the out put power of the engine can be quantified. A very important performance parameter is the effective efficiency which relates the diesel engine work output to the fuel-related heat input. Effective efficiency includes the effect of heat loss, incomplete combustion of the fuel and mechanical losses. Other important performance parameters are fuel consumption, air consumption, air-fuel ratio and air excess ratio.

Power density is an important parameter to express the output of a marine diesel engine in relation to its size or weight. However parameters such as engine speed, mean piston speed and mean effective pressure are influential to power density.

To increase the power output the air has to be forced into the combustion chamber.

Pressure charging is the process of force-feeding air into the combustion chamber of the diesel engine. All marine propulsion diesel engines have an air-charge system with an exhaust driven turbine. This is referred to as turbocharging (patented in 1905 by Dr. Buchi with first practical application in 1923). In chapter2, turbocharging, exhaust gas turbocharger technology and characteristics shall be discussed. However to further increase the density of air, charge air cooling system is provided which cools the compressed air by low temperature water before it is fed into the engine.

In marine propulsion applications the main advantages of diesel engine over other prime movers, is that the diesel engine;

- is relatively insensitive to fuel quality,
- has high reliability,
- has high maintainability due to rather simple technology,
- has high efficiency,
- has relatively lesser initial and operating costs

The disadvantages of the marine diesel engine are its pollutant emissions, when compared to gas turbine, and its low power density.

CHAPTER TWO

Turbocharger technology and selection

2.1 History and milestones

About a half-hour after the invention of the internal combustion engine, somebody figured out that it would make more power if the intake air could be forced into the engine rather than sucked in by the down stroke of the piston. The idea of supplying air under pressure to a diesel engine was voiced by Dr. Rudolf Diesel as early as 1896. Since then, designers and engine manufacturers have been trying to devise new and better ways to stuff cylinders full of mixture for maximum output. Many of these efforts involved crank-driven devices to compress the air, but, a Swiss designer named Dr. Alfred J. Buchi came up with the idea of using exhaust gases to drive the compressor. Dr. A. Buchi filed an application to patent his first turbocharger with Swiss patent office in 1905 and he further patented his so called "pulse system" in 1925. This system feeds the exhaust gases of the engine through narrow pipes to the turbocharger turbine, thus driving the compressor. The pressure variation in the small-volume pipes allows overlapping of the inlet and exhaust, permitting scavenging of the compression space of the engine cylinder with clean air. Cylinders that do not disturb each other's scavenging process can be connected to one pipe (turbine gas inlet) in accordance with the firing order of the diesel engine. This pulse system was the foundation for further success of turbocharging.

In December 1928, following a lecture given by Dr. A. Buchi at the Royal Institute of Engineers at Hague in the Netherlands it was learnt that the thermal load of a diesel engine does not essentially increase when turbocharged. Thus began a phase of extensive research and development.

2.2 Working principle

The development of turbocharged marine diesel engines has always aimed at higher power and efficiency. About 75% of engine power relies on the turbocharger.

The turbocharger consists of two machines (Fig. 2.1), a turbine and a compressor which are mounted on a common shaft. The exhaust gases from the diesel engine flow through the gas inlet casing and nozzle ring to the turbine wheel. The turbine uses the energy contained in the exhaust gas to drive the compressor.

The compressor draws in fresh air and compresses it before being forced into the cylinders. The exhaust gases exit the turbocharger via the gas outlet casing. The turbocharger is gas tight.

The rotating compressor wheel is driven at high speed by the turbine. The air which is necessary for the operation of the diesel engine and which is compressed in the turbocharger is drawn through the suction branch or the silencer into the compressor wheel. Impeller blades accelerate and fling out the air into the diffuser casing at high velocity. It then leaves the turbocharger through the volute of the air outlet housing.

The diffuser transforms the high velocity air into high-pressure air for combustion in the diesel engine.

The rotor runs in two radial plain bearings which are located in the bearing bush between the compressor casing and turbine casing. The axial thrust bearing is on the compressor side. The plain bearings are connected to a central lubricating oil field in which the oil is supplied by the oil system of the diesel engine. The oil outlet is always at the lowest point of the bearing casing.

The turbocharger may be provided with an emergency lubricating oil tank. In the event of failure of the lubricating oil system this emergency lubrication provides a supply of oil to the bearing positions until the rotor stands still.

The power necessary to drive a compressor in the turbocharger must be equal to the power delivered by the turbine. The power of a rotating machine, such as a compressor or a turbine, is:

$$P = \dot{m}.\Delta h = \dot{m}.c_p \Delta T \ (2.1)$$

This relationship shows the direct influence of mass flow on the output of the turbocharger. The temperature drop over the turbine is directly related to the pressure drop.

The pressure drop over the turbine depends on the flow area of the turbine and on the exhaust flow forced by the engine on the turbine. So, the output of the turbocharger mainly depends on the mass flow. [4]

When the same equation is applied to the compressor, it shows that the power input will result not only in a pressure rise, but also in a temperature rise of the charge air.

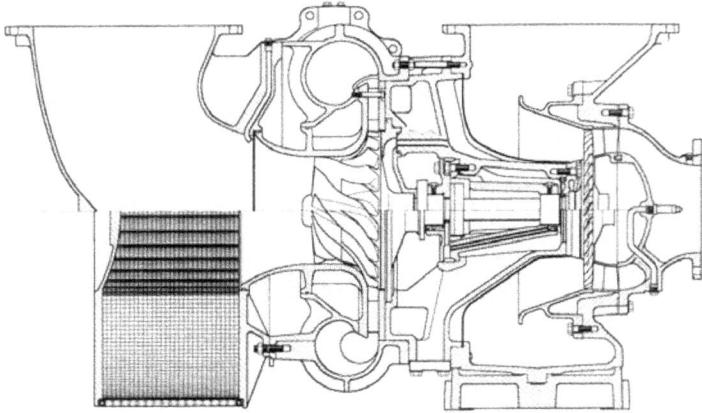

Fig. 2.1: Modern exhaust gas turbocharger [5]

To lower the temperature and to increase the density, a charge air cooler is required between the compressor and the inlet air receiver. This helps to increase the engine output at more moderate charging pressure levels (e.g. a mean effective pressure of ١٠bar, a charging pressure of ٠.٦bar gauge with air-cooler and ٠.٨٥bar without air-cooler, for the same charge of air (kg) in the cylinders; without an air-cooler the exhaust gas temperature would be some ٥٠°C higher).

Essentially, a turbocharged marine diesel engine will exhibit decreasing specific fuel consumption with an increasing degree of turbocharging.

In addition, deeper knowledge of the thermodynamic properties of the diesel process and a better understanding of the fuel injection systems will help to substantially reduce the specific fuel consumption of marine diesel engines.

For comparison, a naturally aspirating diesel engine may have a mean effective pressure of 6 to 7bar and a turbocharged diesel engine of 10 to 30bar, for identical cylinder size.

In addition to above advantages the state of the art for modern marine diesel engines is an output ⸱times (400 percent) as high as the non-turbocharged diesel engine for the same speed and dimensions.

This means that the specific fuel oil consumption of modern turbocharged marine diesel engine amounts to only 80 percent of the specific fuel oil consumption of the non-turbocharged diesel engine. Thus, turbocharged diesel engines are a must in terms of environmental protection, as fuel that is not consumed, neither will cause air pollution, nor produce CO_2. Also, the modern turbocharger combining high pressure ratios with high efficiency is an important factor when the engine process has to be adjusted to achieve a low NO_x emission level through low process temperatures (high air-to-fuel ratio, high charging pressure). Put in general terms, the materials and energy required to produce a turbocharged marine diesel engine for a given output and speed are considerably lower than for a non-turbocharged one for the same output and speed. The advantages of turbo-charging by means of an exhaust gas turbocharger system are:

- A substantial increase in the diesel engine output for a given speed which is approximately proportional to the absolute charging pressure supplied by the turbocharger, for any stated diesel engine size and piston speed, alternatively, a substantial reduction in engine dimensions and weight for any stated horse-power;

- An appreciable reduction in required space for the installation of a specific engine output, with more favorable specific fuel consumption rate at all engine loads;
- Increased reliability and reduced maintenance costs, resulting from less-exacting conditions at cylinders.
- An appreciable reduction in the specific fuel consumption rate at all engine loads;
- A reduction in initial cost;
- Increased reliability and reduced maintenance costs, resulting from less-exacting conditions at cylinders.
- A reduction in harmful diesel engine emissions

2.3 Operating modes

A turbocharger may be operated on the constant-pressure principle or on the pulse principle. The differences between these principles lie in the design of the exhaust system of the diesel engine. Just before the exhaust valve opens, the cylinder process ends with a relatively high pressure and temperature. In the constant pressure system, during blow down, the cylinder pressure drops quickly to the exhaust receiver pressure and the pressure in a large receiver remains almost constant. In the pulse system however the pressure in a relatively small receiver, on the other hand, has a pulsating character.

A constant pressure system features one big exhaust manifold, which collects the exhaust gases of all cylinders. As the mass flow fluctuations caused by the cylinders that intermittently exhaust into the receiver, are dampened out by the sheer size of the manifold, the pressure in the manifold is relatively low and constant over the cycle. [4]

In the pulse system, up to three cylinders are connected to one turbine by a small exhaust pipe. The pressure in the manifold is low, which is advantageous for the scavenging process. Until one of the cylinders opens its exhaust, the pressure rises quickly, even higher than the charge pressure before the engine, giving the turbine a boost. The energy present in the exhaust gases is more effectively transported to the turbine. The pressure before the turbine is high and the blow down losses are much smaller than for the constant pressure system. The greater pressure ratio over the turbine however is counteracted by a lower efficiency of the turbine due to the increased flow losses as a result of the pulsating flow. [4]

2.4 Turbocharger efficiency

2.4.1 Efficiency calculation

The efficiency is an important criterion for the evaluation of the turbocharger. The equation 2.2 shows how the efficiency of turbocharger can be calculated. The specific thermal value " C_p " and the isentropic exponent "k" are temperature dependent. The isentropic exponent for the exhaust gas " k_g " is also influenced by the gas composition. In two-stroke engine, however, the air pressure in the

41

scavenging air pipe plus the cooler pressure drop are used for P_2, while the ambient reduced by the filter losses is used for P_1. The pressure in the exhaust manifold is P_3. The efficiencies are calculated with the help of measured operating values and so when pressure and temperature before the turbine are not known, then it is not possible to determine the turbocharger efficiency. [1]

$$\eta_{TC} = \frac{T_1}{T_2} x \frac{\dot{m}_L}{\dot{m}_g} x \frac{C_{pL}}{C_{pg}} [\frac{(P_2/P_1)^{\frac{K_L-1}{K_L}} - 1}{1 - (P_4/P_3)^{\frac{K_G-1}{K_G}}}] (2.2)$$

$T_1 = CompressorInletTemperature[K]$
$T_3 = TurbineInletTemperature[K]$

$\dot{m}_L = AirMass[kg/s]$

$\dot{m}_g = GasMass(AirandFuelOil[kg/s])$
$C_{pL} = SpecificHeat(air[J/kg.K])$
$C_{pg} = SpecificHeat(gas[J/kg.K])$
$P_1 = AirInlet\,Pr\,essure[bar]$
$P_2 = Ch\arg eAir\,Pr\,essure[bar]$
$P_3 = TurbineInlet\,Pr\,essure[bar]$
$P_4 = TurbineOutlet\,Pr\,essure[bar]$
$k_L = IsentropicExponent(air)$
$k_g = IsentropicExponent(gas)$
$\eta_{TC} = Turboch\arg erEfficiency$
$P_2/P_1 = Pr\,essureRatio(compressor)$
$P_3/P_4 = Pr\,essureRatio(turbine)$

2.4.2 Total (tot – tot)

Total efficiency is one of the most common factors for the thermodynamic characters of turbocharger. Total pressures directly in front and after the compressor and in front of turbine as well as total temperatures are to be put in the equation. The flow velocity in the turbine outlet casing is not taken into account as no further stage for the usage of the dynamic pressure is given; as a result, the static exhaust gas turbine outlet pressure is applied and not the total pressure. [1]

2.4.3 Total-static (tot - stat)

The ambient pressure is used and the losses between compressor outlet and inlet are comprehended in the charge air cooler. As only the static compressor outlet pressure can be used in the engine, and not the dynamic portion, the compressor outlet pressure is used instead of total value. As a result, the ambient pressure at the silencer is applied for P_1 and the static pressure after the turbine is applied for P_2. [1]

2.5 Core technology developments

As with most industrial sectors, turbocharger design and manufacturing businesses are facing constant pressure to enhance products whilst remaining cost competitive. For manufacturers of propulsion marine diesel engines, the turbocharger is a critical component. From a technical standpoint, not only it is a key factor in the engine performance, but it is also critical to overall product reliability.

Additionally the external demands from end users and the progressively more stringent regulatory requirements such as International Maritime Organization (IMO) rules which are demanding reduction in emissions to which both the turbocharger manufacturers and the diesel engine manufacturers have to respond, and increasing pressure ratio requirements resulting from the progression to higher specific cylinder powers, lead to obvious pressures on the manufacturer to continually develop their existing products and introduce enhanced products.

There are currently progressive developments in turbocharger manufacturing process but since it is not possible in the context of this dissertation to cover all the currently underway developments, the following is, however, intended to give an appreciation of how slow speed marine propulsion diesel engine application requirements are placing demands on turbocharger designs; and design and manufacturing initiatives are facilitating the continuous improvement in turbocharger product technology.

2.5.1 Compressor technology

The main parts of the turbocharger compressor are the compressor wheel (inducer and impeller), common rotor and compressor shaft, diffuser, silencer-filter, air intake casing and compressor casing.

2.5.1.1 Compressor wheel and the diffuser

The compressor wheel (Fig.2.2) which is one of the most important parts of the turbocharger is normally made of a single piece high-strength aluminum alloy for compression ratios up to 4.5 and single piece titanium for compression ratios over 4.5.

Fig. 2.2: Optimized aerodynamics compressor wheel [5]

The highly stressed, one piece impeller wheel which withstands the high circumferential velocities of up to 560 m/s, the splitter bladed impeller design, the backswept blades, and the diffuser blades arranged with correct angle of incidence with a profile that reduces the losses caused by collision to a minimum, ensures efficiency as high as 87% in a given design operation range. The enlarged compressor wheel diameter with increased volume flow also exhibits optimized matching of the turbocharger and large propulsion engine. [1]

The compressor wheel which may feature a corrosion resistance coating to protect the impeller against acidic corrosion must fulfill the following requirements:

- To provide the engine with a sufficient amount of air at the desired pressure.
- High compressor efficiency.
- Wide compressor map to ensure a safe surge margin, not only at full load, but also at part load.
- To take high loads due to blades loads as well as centrifugal and vibration stresses.

Fig. 2.3 shows a schematic of a compressor wheel. Assume that the wheel stands still with the space between the blades filled with air at ambient pressure and temperature and then consider a small air mass volume at a radius r.

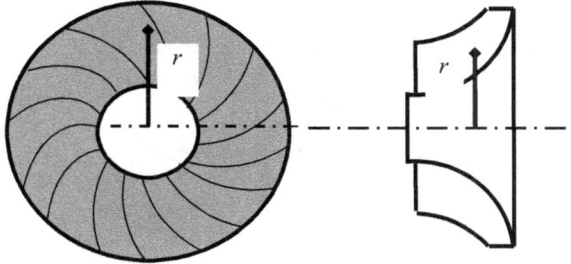

Fig. 2.3: Compressor wheel. Air mass volume at radius r [6]

When compressor wheel starts to rotate (Fig. 2.4) with a circumferential speed U, at radius r, the speed will be V. The small air mass volume will be subjected to a radial acceleration, V^2/r which causes the wheel to move outwards in radial direction. All the air experiences this influence and it begins to flow into the air inlet casing through the compressor wheel and into the diffuser and air outlet casing. The air eventually leaves the compressor wheel at its circumference with an absolute velocity C. It should be noted that the general performance of the compressor is positively influenced by low air friction losses on the various flow surfaces of the compressor wheel and the diffuser. [6]

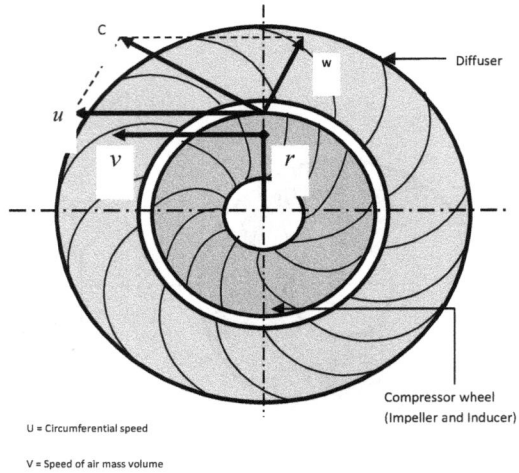

Fig. 2.4: Rotating compressor wheel [6]

2.5.1.2 Compressor characteristic

To determine the specification for a turbocharger compressor, two characteristic variables are required. These accurately establish the operating point in the compressor map (characteristic). For the map representation the variables commonly used by ABB Turbo System Ltd, are [7]:

The total pressure ratio of the compressor:

$$\Pi_{VA}^{*} = P_{VA}^{*} / P_{VE}^{*} \quad (2.3)$$

Where: $P_{VA}^{*} =$ Pressure at compressor outlet under total conditions

$P_{VE}^{*} =$ Pressure at compressor inlet under total conditions

The volumetric flow rate of the compressor in the suction condition, corrected to $15^{O}C(288.15K)$ [7]:

$$\dot{V} = \frac{\dot{m}}{p_{VE}^{*}} \sqrt{\frac{288.15}{T_{VE}^{*}}} = \frac{\dot{m}_{VE}\sqrt{288.15 . T_{VE}^{*}}}{p_{VE}^{*}} \quad (2.4)$$

Where: $\dot{m} =$ mass flow rate and $T_{VE}^{*} =$ temperature at the compressor inlet. These determining variables should be calculated for the nominal operating of the propulsion engine. Additionally a check will always be carried out through out the operating range to see whether any engine or turbocharger limit values are exceeded. Fig. 2.5 shows the characteristic of a modern compressor. [7]

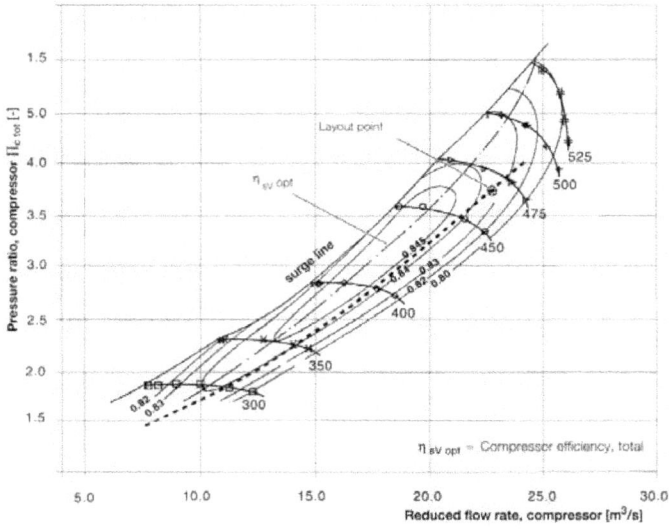

Fig. 2.5 Typical compressor characteristic [1]

At a given speed and with increasing volume, the achievable pressure ratio is lower due to the lower efficiency. The explanation of this can be found in Fig. 2.6.

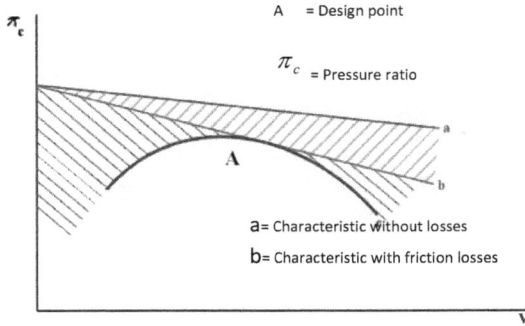

Fig. 2.6 Compressor characteristic with backswept vanes [6]

Theoretically, a compressor with backswept vanes and no losses due to incidence or due to friction will exhibit a decreasing pressure ratio with the increasing volume (line a). But there is friction, and it increases with the volume (line b).

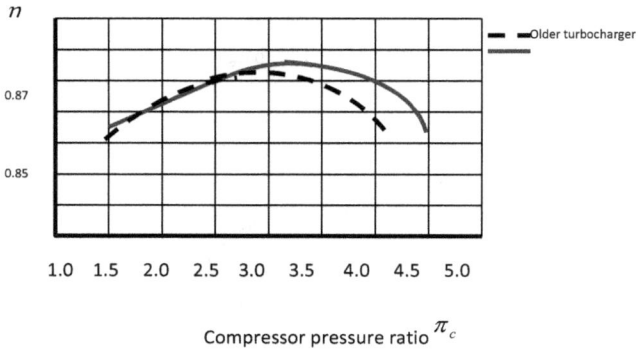

Fig. 2.7: Compressor efficiency on a constant-speed engine operating line versus

To the left and right of design point A on the constant speed line c, the angle of incidence of the flow into the diffuser is not optimal. The hatched areas represent the magnitude of the losses. The progress in achievable pressure ratio and compressor efficiency on a constant speed engine operating line is also shown in the Fig. 2.7.

2.5.1.3 Compressor silencer-air filter

The turbocharger for marine propulsion diesel engine have plate-type silencer as a standard; they are surrounded by an effective air filter. A special guide cone inside the silencer ensures equalization on the air flow and uniform air admission to the compressor.

Silencer features following characteristics:

- Contributes to high turbocharger efficiencies due to their low pressure losses, especially at higher mass flows;
- Effective noise level reduction to the required standard level;
- Maximum velocities of the air at silencer inlet of 6 m/s.

The soft air filter helps to keep compressor, diffuser and intercooler free from deposits by an effective filtering process. [1]

2.5.1.4 Air intake casing

The air inlet casing is either constructed with 90 degree bent or as an axial air inlet duct. The large flow paths and wide-curved deflection regions exhibit constant pressure and velocity distribution at compressor inlet.

2.5.1.5 Compressor outlet casing

The compressor casing which is normally made of grey cast iron, with its wide flow sections and large outlet areas, it ensures efficient conversion of kinetic energy into pressure. In the large propulsion engine where high charge air pressures (continuously above 4.0 bars) are required, the compressor casing can be heat insulated as the classification society requirement or as per request of the buyer, the ship-builder or engine manufacturer.

2.5.2 Turbine technology

2.5.2.1 Turbines design

There are two completely different designs; radial flow and axial flow exhaust gas turbines which are used to drive turbocharger compressors. Radial turbine is normally used in small turbocharger fitted on engine with supercharged engine output from $500\,kW$ to about $4500\,kW$ per turbocharger, where axial turbine is used on propulsion engine (medium-speed and slow-speed engines). The radial turbine is perfectly capable of accepting the exhaust gas from engine running on heavy fuel oil with ability to retain its high efficiency over a very long period of time, especially when reasonable maintenance is provided. [8] The axial turbine is able to supply an adequate output with good efficiency to drive the compressor from low pressure ratios upwards, thus assuring good part-load performance of the engine. The latter is especially important for fixed- pitch propeller drives. Variable turbine geometry with higher part-load boost pressure and improved dynamic response ensures best transient performance and reduces fuel consumption and emissions in engine's part load operation. [8] The main parts of a modern turbocharger turbine are the turbine rotor (disk and rotor blades), common compressor and rotor shaft, nozzle ring, gas admission and gas outlet casings and integrated turbine cleaning device.

2.5.2.2 Turbine characteristic

To determine the specification for turbine, as in the compressor, two characteristic variables are required; these accurately establish the operating point in the turbine map (characteristic). For the map representation the variables commonly used by ABB Turbo System Ltd, are [7]:

- The expansion pressure ratio of the turbine:

$$\Pi_T = P_{TE}^* / P_{TA} \quad (2.5)$$

Where: Π_T is expansion pressure ratio of the turbine (pressure under total conditions at the inlet and under static conditions at the outlet), P_{TE}^* is pressure at turbine inlet under total conditions, and P_{TA} is static pressure at the turbine outlet.

- The effective cross-sectional area of a nozzle having the same flow capacity as the turbine (usually termed the equivalent nozzle area):

$$S_{Teff} = \alpha_{Tgeom} = \frac{\dot{m}_{TE} \sqrt{R_A . T_{TE}^*}}{P_{TE}^* . \Psi_m (\Pi_T, \bar{k}_A)} \quad (2.6)$$

Where: S_{Teff} is the equivalent turbine nozzle area, α_{Tgeom} is reference flow coefficient defined by the turbine geometry, $\dot{m}_{TE}$ is the exhaust gas flow at the turbine inlet, R_A

Is gas constant of the exhaust gas, T_{TE}^{*} is temperature at turbine inlet under total condition, Ψ_m is function for calculating the isentropic mass flow through a nozzle, and $\overline{k}_A$ is mean isentropic exponent of the exhaust gas. As in the compressor case these determining variables should be calculated for the nominal operating of the propulsion engine. Additionally a check will always be carried out through out the operating range to see whether any engine or turbocharger limit values are exceeded. [7]

Figure 2.8 shows the turbine efficiency versus the pressure ratio for three different specifications: full load, intermediate and part load optimization.

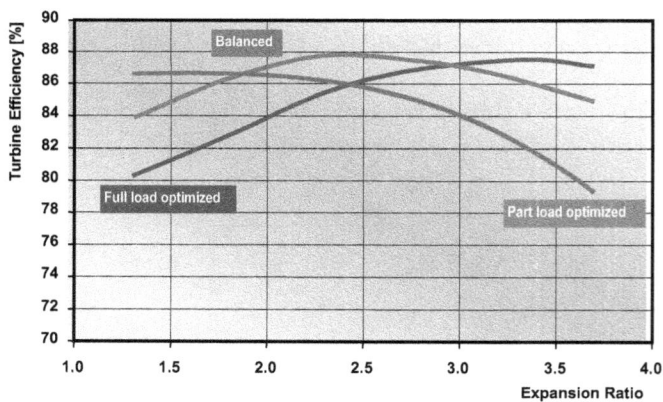

Fig.2.8: Turbine efficiency versus the turbine pressure ratio [1]

2.5.2.3 Turbine rotor

The forged turbine disk (Fig. 2.9) consists of a high-tensile, heat resistance alloy and is connected with the rotor shaft by means of friction welding [1].

Fig. 2.9: Turbine disk [1]

The blades are precisely forged of a Nimonic alloy. The blades are fastened to the turbine disk by means of a fir-tree foot connection. Improved constructively design of the modern turbocharger has made the turbine blades very well accessible for inspection and cleaning with the usual damping wire in the turbine blade ring omitted. [1]

2.5.2.4 Turbine nozzle ring

The cast nozzle ring with profiled blades largely contributes to the excellent efficiency of the turbine. With improved flow in the nozzle ring, the vibration acceleration of the rotor blades is reduced and at the same time the stability of the nozzle ring is remarkably improved, especially when it is subjected to heavy stress from cleaning granulates. The casings if insulated with simple and highly efficient insulation material, they guarantee a lower noise level as well as low surface temperature in the engine room. [1]

2.5.2.5 Turbine casing

The gas admission and gas outlet casings having wide flow areas are made of nodular iron, and with improved constructively design they are un-cooled and are effectively insulated with the flow losses minimized. Since the turbine outlet casing flange may be subject to loads by the effected gas forces, additional exterior forces and or torque and the gas admission casing flange unlike the turbine outlet casing may be subject only to loads by the effected gas forces, this necessitates the use of compensators directly at the turbine inlet and at the turbine outlet. The compensators are to be pre-loaded in such a manner that thermal expansion of the pipes and the casing do not affect force or torque in addition to the gas forces. [1]

2.5.3 Cleaning device

In modern turbocharger where efficient and standard synthetic air filter is normally used the washing of compressor can be dispensed, provided the air filter is properly treated. However turbocharger's turbine must be cleaned at regular intervals beginning from the very first operation to remove combustion residues from the blades of rotor and nozzle ring, failure to do so might cause a deterioration of the operating data or severe excitations of the rotor blades. Two principal cleaning procedures for turbine are: Turbine wet cleaning and turbine dry cleaning. Both cleaning methods can be used with the same turbocharger to complement the advantages of each single device.

In wet cleaning fresh water free from any chemical additives with approximate pressure of 3 bars has to be used and in order to avoid overload on turbine blades by thermo-shock and centrifugal stresses, the propulsion engine load has to be reduced to 10% of normal load.

In dry cleaning with advantage of carrying it out during normal operation of the engine, the container for the granulate matter has to be filled with the maker's specified quantity and has to be blown-in during an injection period of approximately 30 seconds.

2.5.4 Bearing Technology

2.5.4.1 Bearing design

Modern turbochargers which are designed for operation with engine lubricating oil with required filtration of about 5o μm filter mesh size, demand, high-tech bearing technology (Fig.2.10) to guarantee safe and reliable turbocharger operation under all circumstances. Therefore such bearings features should include the axial thrust bearing with the free floating disc for high loads and high speeds, and the radial fixed bearing bushes, centered in a squeeze oil damper.

The axial floating disc rotates at about half of the rotor speed between the rotating and static thrust bearing components. By this design the relative velocities are reduced to cause better oil film formation and declination tolerance and prolongs the bearing lifetime.

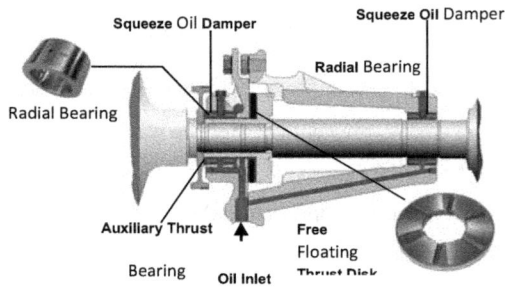

Fig. 2.10: Axial thrust and radial bearings location [5]

Plain bearings of inboard arrangement, made of steel back, cast of stannous, lead and bronze alloy material, designed in a multi-lobe geometry, to ensure centering of the rotor shaft. The bearing on the compressor side takes both axial and radial forces where as the bearing on the rotor side takes radial forces only. The turbine side bearing is designed as floating bearing bush to ensure quiet running even at the highest speeds [5].

The inboard bearing arrangement resulted in:

- Ideal axial admission of the air to the compressor wheel and of the exhaust gases to the nozzle ring and the turbine
- Short bearing distance therefore exact alignment of the rotor, critical rotor speeds outside the operating speed range
- Short and stiff rotor with low moment of inertia, therefore good acceleration response
- Excellent access to all bladed components for inspection and maintenance

The advantages of the plain bearings are:

- Long life time
- Ideal behavior at very high axial and radial forces
- High damping effect due to large hydraulic oil film
- Insensitive to vibrations and imbalances
- No necessity for vibration control

2.5.4.2 Bearing lubrication

During the normal operation of the turbocharger the bearings are lubricated via the main engine lubricating oil system (Fig. 2.11).

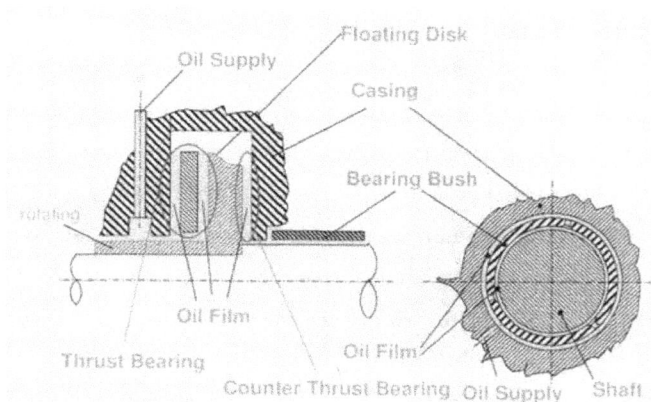

Fig. 2.11: Bearing lubrication [5]

At the same time the emergency lubricating oil tank is continuously filled with system oil via a small bypass bore in the non-return valve with excess lube oil being supplied to the engine's lube oil circuit by means of free overflow.

In the event of disturbance in lubricating oil supply, the integrated emergency oil tank on the turbocharger secures a safe rotor run down. If the oil supply is disturbed because of e.g. a black out, there will be more than sufficient amount of oil within the emergency oil system (Fig. 2.12) to secure bearing lubrication after engine shut down. Since the emergency oil system employs the principle of pure gravity, this simple system does not require any auxiliaries.

Fig. 2.12: Emergency bearing lubrication [5]

2.5.4.3 Bearing casing

Modern turbochargers use completely water-free heat insulated bearing casings made of cast iron, machined in one single setting resulting in an uniquely exact rotor alignment which can be withdrawn (with complete rotating assembly) from the turbine housing without need to disconnect exhaust manifolds to and from engine.

2.5.5 Sealing air system

The sealing air prevents the penetration of hot exhaust gas into the bearing casing and lube oil from seeping into turbine (Fig. 2.13). It also helps to reduce undesired thrust on the axial bearing disc. The sealing air system is fully integrated in the bearing casing without ruling out the option for the turbocharger to also be operated with external sealing air. A part of the air compressed by the compressor wheel is diverted and flows out of the compressor casing into a ring duct in the bearing casing. From there the air is led into the sealing air pipe, whereby an orifice reduces the pressure to the required sealing air pressure. The air is led to a ring duct on the turbine side of the bearing casing. There the sealing air emerges between shaft and turbine labyrinth where, a small amount of the sealing air flows back into the bearing casing via the labyrinth rings and thus holds back the lubricating oil, and the other part of the sealing air is led past the turbine disk into the gas outlet casing.

The sealing air pressure is factory set via the orifice and there are no needs to either control it or adjust it by the end user [1].

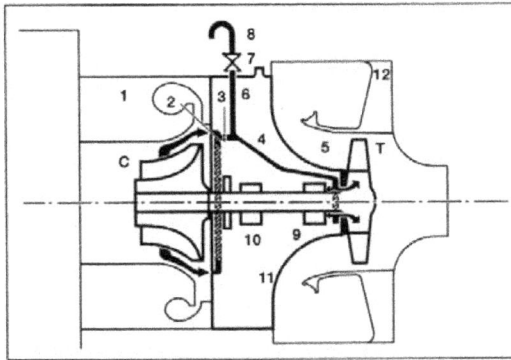

Fig. 2.13: Sealing air diagram [1]

01- Compressor casing

02- Ring duct, compressor side

03- Orifice

04- Sealing air pipe

05- Ring duct, turbine side

06- Compensation pipe

07- Non-return valve

08- Pipe bend

09- Bearing bush

10- Locating bearing

11- Bearing casing

12- Gas outlet casing

2.6 Other issues

2.6.1 Vibration

Any vibratory forces or couples that may emanate from a main engine "diesel propulsion plant" under consideration must be carefully assessed before it is accepted as suitable. [9] It is often the case that much effort is correctly directed towards core improvements offering higher performance and higher efficiencies. Manufacturers, however, have also kept in perspective all application requirements, some of which are associated immediately with the diesel engine needs and some driven by the market and by legislation. One such issue is that of vibration levels. Natural frequencies of rotating components are nowadays always analyzed in the design phase. It is also important, however, that the natural frequency of the turbocharger assembly should be thoroughly evaluated and the overall system response of the turbocharger on its bracket understood. In addition to theoretical analyses, the vibration characteristics of turbochargers and their air filter silencers have been practically evaluated on a shaker table to give confidence in the natural frequencies being well above any exciting frequencies from the diesel engine. [9] The turbocharger and air filter silencers assemblies may additionally be analyzed on the diesel engine bracket to further assist understanding of the system as a whole and to provide sound data to support theory. This work can ultimately result in more reliable modeling of the turbocharger and air filter silencers in order to prevent vibration problems being encountered in service.

2.6.2 Noise emissions and control

The market leaders in marine two stroke diesel propulsion plant are in no doubt that the rising tide of environmental awareness and controls, hitherto mainly expressed in exhaust emission controls, will necessitate new technical initiatives as regards engine-emitted noise. Greater demands are accordingly being placed on engine designers to provide more detailed and precise information regarding noise emissions and its various forms. One of the main origins of noise emissions from two-stroke machinery is the turbocharger. [10]

The charging systems of large marine diesel engines comprise up to four turbochargers. The components connected to the turbocharger can contribute considerably to the total noise level of the engine. In particular, these components are mainly responsible for pure tone noise transmitted from the compressor outlet. The result of development work for reducing noise at the compressor outlet revealed that an acoustically optimized diffuser is highly effective in reducing the noise level at the compressor outlet. [11]

As mentioned earlier the increasing demands with respect to the diesel engine output required increased pressure ratio and volume flow of the turbochargers, which has resulted in higher noise emissions. Therefore noise attenuation and the noise level produced by the turbocharger is also a subject of close scrutiny. Legislation continues to improve the safety and comfort of working environments and noise exposure is one key element of this. Current standards dictate the need for noise levels of typically $110\,dB(A)$ or NR 105 at 1m. It is likely that levels will further reduce and there will be a need to further improve attenuation in this respect. Development work is therefore proceeding on variations in design, which will allow these criteria to be met.

Typical sound power limits on ships measured at a distance of 1 meter from the engine are $110\,dB(A)$ for 100 percent load or $105\,dB(A)$ at slightly reduced load. Turbochargers being capable of operating over a wide range of gas flows and power ratings generate noise with complex mechanism, possess both body-radiated and aerodynamic noise source. Attempts at separately quantify the generated noise within a turbocharger are complex too, particularly with respect to turbine exhaust noise, due to extreme temperatures, high exit velocities and products of combustion, etc. The surface sound pressure level of the turbochargers can be calculated from the sound power level which is the energetic sum of the components' partial sound power. That means that for a prototype turbocharger a sound power level of $113\,dB(A)$ corresponds to a surface sound pressure level of $95\,dB(A)$. Table 2.1 shows the sound power level of the turbocharger components and their respective contribution to the total sound power level.

	Sound power level $dB(A)$
Turbocharger overall	**121.8**
Silencer circumference plus front area	113.3
Compressor scroll	120.5
Turbine casing with standard insulation	112.5

Table 2.1 Component emission level of prototype turbocharger [11]

When comparing these values with a given reference value of the total sound power level of $113\,dB(A)$ it is easy to ascertain which components actually offered potential for improvement i.e. the compressor scroll accounted for the largest percentage of the total, followed by the silencer.

In an attempt by turbocharger designer the enhancement of the silencer design, improvement of the insulation material and introduction of newly designed acoustically optimized diffuser proved to be highly effective in reducing the noise level in the prototype turbocharger (Table 2.2).

	Sound power level $dB(A)$
Turbocharger overall	114.0
Silencer circumference plus front area	111.0
Compressor scroll	110.4
Turbine casing with standard insulation	102.0

Table2.2 Component emission level of prototype turbocharger after modification [11]

2.6.3 Oil cocking

To avoid oil cocking at high gas inlet temperatures or after a shutdown from full load, temperature have to be kept as low possible. This can be achieved by either using water cooled bearing casing or by separation of the bearing bush from the bearing housing.

2.6.4 Containment

To protect personnel and to avoid any risk of injury in the case of turbocharger over speed with sudden break of the connection between the compressor and the shaft all housings are designed to be capable of containing any bursting parts [5].

2.6.5 The surging phenomenon

2.6.5.1 Computational surge stability test

The compressor runs at constant speed and supplies air to the air receiver of the engine, where a required pressure must be maintained. Fig. 1 shows the line of constant speed and the operating line of the engine. The intersection of the two lines is the working point A. If a slight increase in air volume occurs, more pressure is required on the operating line and the pressure becomes lower on the constant speed line. The volume has to decrease again to the point of equilibrium A. If, at the same charger speed, a slight reduction in air flow occurs, the pressure will increase although less pressure is required on the working line. Equilibrium is then once more at point A. The working point A is stable on the part of the constant speed line inclined downwards with increasing volume. If a slight decrease in volume occurs at point B (at the same pressure as A), then the pressure on the constant speed line decreases. The compressor cannot maintain the required pressure, the volume continuous to decrease, and the compressor surges. Point B is not stable on that part of the constant speed line that is inclined upwards (with increasing volume).

Theoretically, instability of the compressor starts where the line of constant speed is level. Since a turbocharger, which supplies a continuous airflow is combined with an engine taking air intermittently; there will always be a pressure fluctuation which influences the point where instability starts. [6]

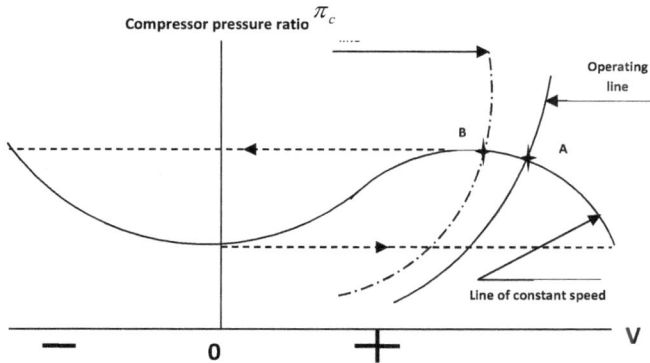

Fig. 2.14: Surging cycle [6]

As per review result of the modern turbochargers specifications the possibility of surging is virtually excluded. It is however always likely for surging to happen after some years of service with maintenance not carried out in accordance with the manufacturer instructions.

The transient operation of a large propulsion engine with constant pressure turbo-charging, where two or more turbochargers supply air in parallel to a common receiver, during turbocharger compressor surging can be investigated through simulation in which a detailed zero-

71

dimensional performance prediction code for reciprocating engines can be used in conjunction with a model capable of predicting the dynamic behavior of the compressor. Steady state as well as transient simulation runs can be performed with the valid results against the experimental data.

Following is the result of an actual experiment performed regarding the examination of the behavior of a large, propulsion engine by employing a detailed zero-dimensional engine simulation code in conjunction with a model capable of predicting compressor surging.

Initially, steady state simulation runs were performed and the derived results were validated against the engine shop trials. Then, a case of engine transient operation at full speed was also examined. The measured ordered engine speed and propeller load were used as input and transient runs were performed in order to determine the engine PI speed governor constants. After determining the governor constants, the predicted transient simulation results were in very good agreement with the data measured in the shipboard tests. Having validated the simulation code against steady state and transient measured data, a case of engine operation with turbocharger compressor surging was simulated. To induce the compressor surging, the turbine of the one of the three turbochargers was considered to be dirty and the turbine swallowing capacity and efficiency were considered 10% lower than the ones of the clean turbine. The surging of compressor caused reduction in the scavenging receiver pressure, which, in turn, resulted in less air available for combustion into the engine cylinders, reduction of engine developed torque and finally drop of engine speed as the engine load almost remained constant. The lack of air for combustion also caused the increase of the exhaust receiver temperature, thus increasing engine thermal loading. In addition, the almost instant changes of the compressor absorbed torque during compressor surging were shown to introduce severe transient torsion loading to the turbocharger shaft. [6]

2.6.5.2 Actual surge stability test

For surge stability test of an installed 2-stroke propulsion engine one of the following methods can also be adopted:

1. Run the engine at 100% load. Reduce the load suddenly to about 75%. If no surging occurs repeat the process, this time reducing the load from 100% to 50% load. If no surging occurs, the stability above 50% load is good.

2. Run the engine at part load with a charge air pressure of about 0.6 bar gauge. Pull the fuel pump of one cylinder, suddenly to zero. Repeat this test with other cylinders. If surging occurs in one case, the stability is acceptable.

2.6.6 Fuels

In vast majority of engines, the burning of fuel is the prerequisite of thermodynamic process, so it is important to understand the chemical reactions which take place during combustion. In many chemical reactions energy is liberated; in others energy is absorbed. A chemical reaction in which energy is absorbed is called an endothermic reaction. A chemical reaction in which energy is liberated is called an exothermic reaction. Thus fuel-burning reactions are exothermic reactions. [12]

The quality of the fuel which the engine is operated affects the composition of the exhaust gas. Impurities in the fuel can lead to residue in the exhaust gas which can affect the engine parts and the turbocharger in an abrasive or corrosive manner.

All modern two-stroke engines can run on crude-oil based heavy fuel oil (HFO), when engine and processing system are designed accordingly. The fuels used must meet the respective limit values that are listed in the fuel specifications. The limit values that influence the engine operation are normally specified when ordering fuel.

Adding motor lubricants (waste oil), mineral oil, foreign material such as coal oil and remainders from refining or other processes (e.g. solvent) is banned and not yet part of the standard. Such additions lead to combustion with high residue and increased wear and corrosion on the parts and components in way of exhaust gas flow. Adding motor lubricants (waste oil) is particularly critical as the lube oil additives cause emulsions to form and keep debris, water and catalyst particles finely distributed in poise. This impedes or avoids the required fuel cleaning.

ISO 8217 GRADE			RMA10	RMD15	RME25	RMG35	RMH45 RMH55
CHARACTERISTIC	Unit	Limit					
density@15 $\dot{\circ}$C	Kg/m³	Max	975	985	991	991	991
Kinematic Visc.@100$\dot{\circ}$ C	cSt	Max	10	15	25	35	45
Approx Visc.@ 50$\dot{\circ}$ C**	cSt		50	100	225	390	585
Flash Point	$\dot{\circ}$C	Min	60	60	60	60	60
Pour Point, Winter	$\dot{\circ}$C	Max	0	30	30	30	30
Pour Point, Summer	$\dot{\circ}$C	Max	6	30	30	30	30
Micro Carbon Residue	%m/m	Max	10	14	15	18	22
Ash	%m/m	Max	0.10	0.10	0.10	0.15	0.20
Water	%V/V	Max	0.5	0.8	1.0	1.0	1.0
Sulphur	%m/m	Max	3.5	4.0	5.0	5.0	5.0
Vanadium	Mg/kg	Max	150	350	200	300	600
Aluminium+Silicon	Mg/kg	Max	80	80	80	80	80
Total sediment Potential	%m/m	Max	0.10	0.10	0.10	0.10	0.10

Table 2.3: ISO Fuel Standard 8217: 1996(E), Selected Marine Residual Fuels (Class F) Requirements [13]

** Note Approximate Viscosity at 50 degree C as indicated in ISO 8217:1996 Annex C.

---- = No Specified Limit.

The following points are to be observed when thorough processing of heavy fuel is required for trouble free propulsion engine operation:

1. Heavily abrasive inorganic, solid foreign substances (cat-fines, rust and sand) must be separated to the greatest possible extent.

2. Aluminium content greater than 10 mg/kg the abrasive wear in the parts and components in way of exhaust gas flow increases heavily

3. Modern separators of latest generation which are fully capable and effective over a large density range without any adjustment, and separate water with an HFO density of 1.01g/ml at $15°$ C with the cleaning effect by the separator itself, are to be used.

4. The HFO purification is to be designed in such a manner that inorganic solid foreign particle size to be less than 5 μm with an amount less than 20mg/kg and also to lower the water content in the fuel to less than 0.2vol.%.

5. With unfavourable vanadium-sodium ratio, the melting temperature of the HFO ash drops to the range of the exhaust valve temperature, which causes hot corrosion. By pre-cleaning the HFO in the settling tank and in the centrifugal separators, the water and thus the water soluble-sodium compound can be removed to the largest extent. With a sodium content exceeding 100mg/kg, increasing salt deposits in the parts and components in way of exhaust gas flow are to be expected. This may jeopardize the engine operation. However under certain

conditions hot corrosion may be avoided with fuel additives that increase the melting temperature of the HFO ash.

6. Heavy fuel oil with high ash content in form of foreign substances e.g. sand, rust, cat-fines, increase the mechanical wear in the components and parts in way of exhaust gas flow. Heavy fuel oil from catalytic cracking plants can contain cat-fines. There are significant variations from refinery to refinery in the proportion of the aluminium and silicon compounds that comprise catalyst fines. The catalyst fines generally affect high wear in parts and components which are in way of exhaust gas flow. [13]

2.7 Conclusions

The definition and purpose of turbocharging is that exhaust gas can be put to use as an effective resource to achieve greater power, reduced specific fuel consumption, better energy resources conservation, improved performance in environmental impact, and lower costs. The end users demand progress towards ever higher power outputs, and matching turbocharger to diesel engine performance, the external influences of environmental and pollution concerns, and standards laid down by the IMO, classification societies and other concerned bodies in pursuit of more efficient, better performing turbochargers in marine propulsion plants leaves the manufacturer with one choice of designing production processes effective and as efficient as possible. So far there have been many schemes produced over the years involving some complex air charging arrangements. These include turbo-compounding and supercharging arrangements. As always; there are specific applications where these more complex systems can be attractive. For marine drive purposes, however, whether the complexity of such system is appropriate has to be questioned. Although it is not possible to state with certainty where the future lies, it is perhaps instructive to look at present turbocharger designs and consider their conceptual simplicity. High efficiencies are already being achieved with fundamentally simple designs with reduced numbers of the components. If turbo-charging systems become more complex, greater efforts need to be made to ensure reliability is maintained, as it is unlikely that diesel engine manufacturers and operators will tolerate reduced reliability. However for this reason the common approach of the manufacturers is a 'minimalist' approach derived from the trend towards 'pipe less diesel engines'. Typical of this is the range of turbochargers that has simple, modular design, aimed at improving overall life cycle costs. Developments in component design and material all contribute to this goal.

The key design criteria of a modern turbocharger should include:

- High compressor pressure ratio;
- High performance level especially at high pressure ratios;
- High specific flow capacity;
- Reduced fuel oil consumption and less emission of harmful exhaust gases;
- High reliability;
- Highly qualified mechanically

- Enhanced operation safety;
- Robust, simple and compact construction with reduced number of parts;
- Long lifetime;
- Easy maintenance even under adverse condition such as operation with low quality heavy fuel oil;
- Increased time between overhauls;
- Improved allowable vibration acceleration;
- Reduced sound emission values; and
- Improved surge stability

The modern turbocharger is a one-piece system, with both turbine and compressor built onto the same shaft, with inlet air filter systems and connection to the exhaust and charge air manifolds. It is driven by the exhaust gases of the diesel engine flowing through the compressor stage and outputting to the charge air manifold of the engine. In such turbocharger, the plain bearings are designed for about 50-micron mesh size filtration and direct lubrication from the engine's oil supply. The axial thrust bearing uses a free-floating disc, with non-rotating bearing bushes in an oil-squeeze damper. The purpose of the free-floating disc and bearing arrangement is to improve wear resistance, with thicker oil films, when using contaminated oil. As the progress towards ever higher power outputs, and matching turbocharger to engine performance, plus concentration on detailed changes in component design, and increasing the range and capacity of existing designs, will continue, the makers of turbocharger however, accordingly will focus on improvements in the design and operation of the turbocharger, including choice of materials in turbine and compressor units, sealing system, and washing techniques, etc.

Perhaps the most interesting question, however, is where and how turbo-charging will progress in the future and how manufacturers can lead or even create the market for advanced products. It is difficult to predict where the diesel engine manufacturer will move, or even how fast, but the likelihood is that pressure ratios will continue to increase in the drive towards higher ratings and power densities. As such, Titanium impellers are likely to become progressively more commonplace in demanding applications. Titanium impellers offer a means by which simple single stage turbo charging can progress into the immediate future. Having concentrated on the impeller, however, it should be noted that there is a limit to what can be effectively achieved with single stage turbines. From a materials perspective, higher stresses can be accommodated through using improved materials.

In connection with plans for changes to component design and material, the followings may be a center of attention for the makers;

- Provision of an optional nozzle ring capable of adjustment during operation, by the makers of turbocharger.
- The use of ceramic and other coatings to improve the turbocharger's performance and overall life cycle costs by reducing cleaning and maintenance intervals.
- Utilization of polymers and some other materials which are not normally used for turbocharger sealing, to improve the turbocharger sealing systems.

- Increasing thermal efficiency and recovery of the useful, potential source of energy in the diesel engine exhaust gas.

Should the recent escalation of the fuel prices continue, marine diesel engine makers will have to positively react to the end user's demands about saving fuel cost and reduction in emissions, via investment to be put into reducing engine fuel consumption as they did after the 1973 fuel crisis. There is a natural trade-off between diesel engine fuel consumption and NO_X emissions. Reduction in specific fuel consumption involves a natural increase in NO_X emissions. It is also to be remembered that modern large, slow-speed marine diesel engines are very highly developed and there is a little potential for achieving significant reduction in CO_2 emissions by diesel engine development alone thus utilization of wasted energy, may be considered as one of the practical solutions to the problem. In the diesel engines' exhaust gases about 25% of input energy is available at a fairly high temperature which are useful, potential source of energy for recovery process. Since large marine propulsion diesel engines are designed for intake air temperature up to $45^O C$ (intake from engine room) for tropical conditions, the turbocharger can be re-matched to return thermal load of the engine back down to what prevails for the intake temperature at $45^O C$. When considering such a tuning to reach an increased exhaust gas temperature, it is important that the thermal load of the adopted diesel engine should not increase to a level that may jeopardize the diesel engine reliability. Modern, high-efficiency turbochargers also have a small surplus in efficiency capability in the upper load ranges because of which a certain exhaust gas flow can be branched off before the turbocharger to drive a power turbine.

It is always possible that as yet unforeseen developments will change the direction of marine diesel engine and turbocharger development, however, increased power density can surely only be achieved through higher cylinder pressures. At some point, therefore, a change may be likely to occur in turbocharger design and complexity. This is an interesting point to consider, as with increased complexity, the turbocharger will be likely to further increase in cost compared to the diesel engine itself and thus become an even greater center of attention in the overall power package design.

In technology terms, higher pressure ratios are readily achievable but the market for turbocharger has the other demands on it, as have already been indicated, such as size, cost and efficiency. A compact turbocharger "module", with incorporation of inter-cooling, may provide greater flexibility and prove attractive to the market, provided costs can be controlled.

As the public interest focuses on the improved fuel economy, and the environmental acceptability of marine propulsion systems, the minimization of pollutant emissions has to be considered too. So the external influences of environmental and pollution concerns, and standards laid down by the IMO, classification societies and others in pursuit of more efficient, better performing turbochargers in marine propulsion diesel engine plants remains paramount.

CHAPTER 3

Turbocharger matching

3.1 Formulation of the problem

Today turbochargers are normally constructed in series, and in order to adopt the products to any engine with its individual turbo charging system, its output data and installation conditions, turbochargers are constructed according to a modular system. Therefore the following need to be determined for each engine with its turbo charging system, its output data and its ambient conditions:

- Type of turbocharger
- Size of turbocharger
- Number of turbochargers on the same engine
- Specification of the casing variants and positions, the rotor and stator blades arrangements of the compressor and turbine and variants of the bearings and lubricating system

3.2 The method of calculation for matching turbocharger

There are numerous methods for calculating the operating characteristic variables of turbocharged marine diesel engines. They extend from simple, empirical rules for establishing variables required for turbocharger matching, to complicated, programmed procedures by which the real working cycle can be simulated in all its details. An engineer who is concerned with the development of turbo charging systems and the design of exhaust gas turbochargers must, however, be familiar with a method which is appropriate to each task, to enable the best choice to be made for each particular case. [14]

One of the leading turbocharger manufacturers have developed on the basis of years of practical experience, a simple, semi-empirical method of calculation for matching turbochargers. In this method following are considered:

Since as a rule only single turbochargers or small series of machines are ordered to the same design data, the number of design calculations is very large. The cost of each computation must therefore be kept as low as possible. The number of available types, sizes and specifications is also very large. Correspondingly large is the number of compressor and turbine characteristics and the supplementary calculation information. Therefore appropriate representation of this information, and also easily used storage with ready access, is of importance. [7]

Since a particular problem arises from the different turbocharging systems of the various marine type two-stroke diesel engines for which it is not possible to use one consistent mathematical model of the turbocharged engine, the type and quantity of the information and data that the diesel engine manufacturers make available varies considerably, achievement of their specifications and expectations in regard to turbocharger matching and the operating characteristic values is essential. [7]

Since the only measurements that are in general available from test results on turbocharged engines are those that have been obtained from acceptance tests, test runs of ships and turbocharger matching tests, the characteristic values obtained from experience that are used in the computation method must be defined in such a way that they can be determined clearly and with sufficient accuracy from the readings that have been obtained in the usual way. [7]

So, over the years, reliable figures based on experience are made obtainable from the systematically collected and evaluated readings of numerous different propulsion diesel engine plant performances.

A further source of empirical values are detailed studies and tests on turbo charging systems, computer simulations of the exhaust gas exchange and working cycles, which the maker carry out in the course of their continued development of turbocharger technology.

3.3 Modeling and simulation methodology

In proven engineering practice devices are designed, manufactured, and constructed by technologies that are proven by tests and experience, which are reflected in approved codes and standards and other appropriately documented statements, and that are implemented by proper selection and training of qualified persons. [15]

Modeling is the process of identifying the principal physical dynamics effects to be considered in analyzing a system, writing the differential and algebraic equations from the conservation laws and property laws of the relevant discipline, and reducing the equations to a conventional differential equation form. The major disciplines of engineering systems are mechanics, electricity and electronics, fluid mechanics and fluid control, and thermodynamics. [16]

The performance of the diesel engine used in a marine propulsion plant can be predicted from module of a detailed propulsion plant performance prediction code which has been under continuous development for years at the laboratory.

The engine model can be a 'control volume' (filling and emptying) type model that calculates the in-cylinder processes in a degree to degree crank angle resolution. A turbocharged engine is modeled as a several flow receiver elements (control volumes) interconnected by flow controller elements. The flow receiver elements are the cylinders, the scavenging receiver and the exhaust receiver, while the scavenging ports, the exhaust valves, the compressors and the turbines are considered to be the flow controller elements. The engine environment is regarded as a fixed fluid element (constant pressure, temperature and composition).

The flow receivers are treated as open thermodynamic systems, where work, heat and mass transfer take place across the boundaries. The working medium in each flow receiver is regarded as a homogenous mixture of pure air and combustion products, subjected to the perfect gas law. Spatial uniformity of the medium properties is assumed at any instant. Thus, the instantaneous state of the flow receiver gas is described by its pressure, temperature and equivalence ratio. By applying the first law of thermodynamics (energy equation) and the conservation of mass to each flow receiver, the differential equations for the calculation of temperature and mass are derived. The rate of change of a flow receiver gas equivalence ratio with respect to time depends on the rate of fuel addition by injection and on the fuel content

88

in the form of combustion products of the gas entering or exiting the flow receiver.

Simulation procedure includes two distinct phases of operation:

- The steady state phase, and the;
- The transient phase

During the steady state phase (typically used for steady-state performance predictions), the engine is considered to operate under 'frozen' RPM and fixed load with constant fuelling. The program then, by performing a number of cycles, tries to reach a converged solution, implying an equilibrium state of the engine, for all the elements present in the engine configuration. During the transient phase, the program performs the simulation in the time domain. The engine operates under a pre-specified load profile, which may be either constant or variable in time.

The model can predict both the variation of micro-parameters (such as the in-cylinder pressures and temperatures throughout an engine cycle), and the cumulative macro-parameters (such as heat loss, mean effective pressure) in detail for various engine configuration.

3.4 The turbocharger matching procedure

All computation methods for turbocharger matching are essentially meant for selection of the optimum specification. The sequence of the individual procedural steps and the methods and aids used within these steps can, however, vary very considerably according to the turbo charging system and the available information.

Fig. 3.1 illustrates the procedure in the case of a two-stroke diesel engine with constant-pressure turbo charging. Although the procedure has proved its value countless times in practice, its use is nevertheless not obligatory.

The first step in the selection of turbocharger to be matched to large marine slow-speed two-stroke diesel engine is always the procurement of the necessary data and information about the diesel engine, the plant and all the turbochargers concerned, and also their specifications. The more complex and truly representative the computing models are, the more comprehensive this data becomes and the more difficult it is to obtain. Even for the simple, semi-empirical design method set out here, an imposing list of information as stipulated in section 3.3.1 (table of necessary information for turbocharger matching), is required. Additionally for the step-by- step computation of the real working cycle on the computer, a great deal of additional information would also be required. [7]

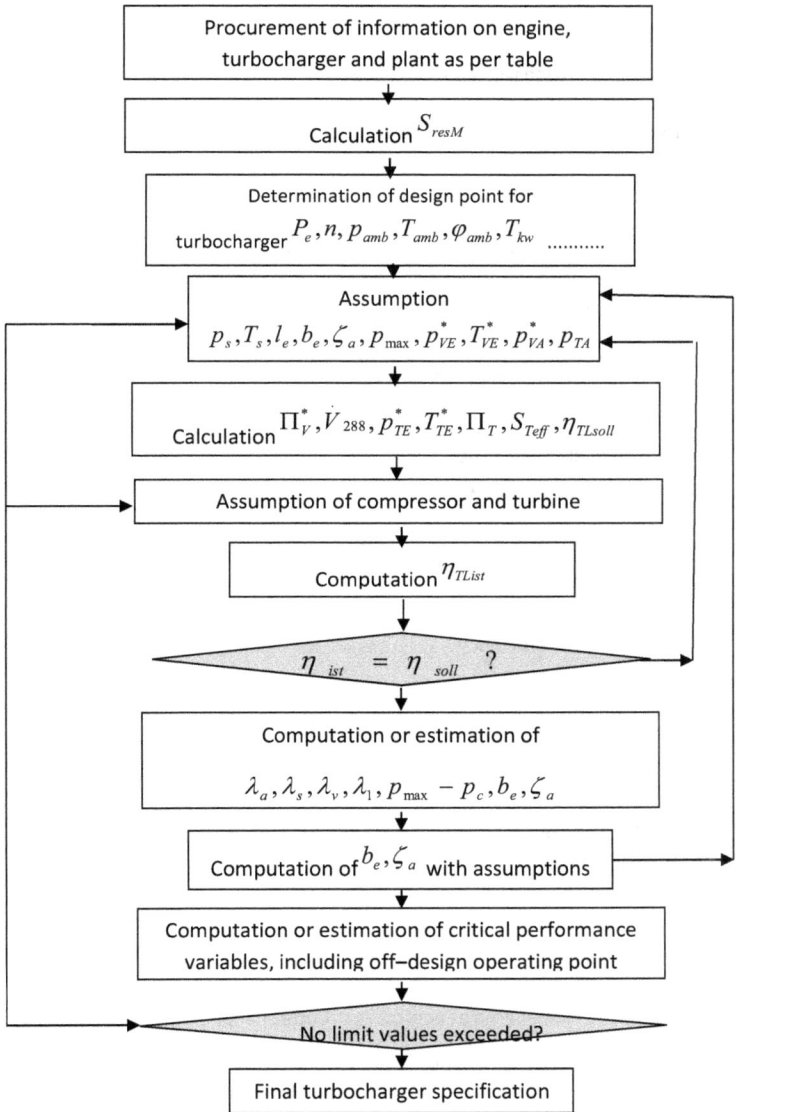

Procurement of information on engine, turbocharger and plant as per table

↓

Calculation S_{resM}

↓

Determination of design point for turbocharger $P_e, n, p_{amb}, T_{amb}, \varphi_{amb}, T_{kw}$ ....

↓

Assumption $p_s, T_s, l_e, b_e, \zeta_a, p_{max}, p_{VE}^*, T_{VE}^*, p_{VA}^*, p_{TA}$

↓

Calculation $\Pi_V^*, \dot{V}_{288}, p_{TE}^*, T_{TE}^*, \Pi_T, S_{Teff}, \eta_{TLsoll}$

↓

Assumption of compressor and turbine

↓

Computation η_{TList}

↓

$\eta_{ist} = \eta_{soll}$?

↓

Computation or estimation of $\lambda_a, \lambda_s, \lambda_v, \lambda_1, p_{max} - p_c, b_e, \zeta_a$

↓

Computation of b_e, ζ_a with assumptions

↓

Computation or estimation of critical performance variables, including off–design operating point

↓

No limit values exceeded?

↓

Final turbocharger specification

91

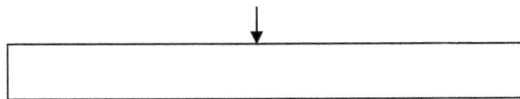

Fig. 3.1: Flow diagram for turbocharger matching to a two-stroke diesel engine with constant pressure charging [7]

3.4.1 The necessary information for turbocharger matching

A- Turbocharger computing information

For all types, sizes and specifications the following are required:

- Compressor characteristics

$$\eta_{sV}^* = \eta_{sV}^* \, (\dot{V}_{288}, \, \Pi_v^*) \; [7] \qquad (3.1)$$

- Turbine characteristics

$$\eta_{sT}^* = \eta_{sT}^* \, (\Pi_T, u/c_0) \; [7] \qquad (3.2)$$

Additional information:

- Volumetric efficiency η_{vol} (allows for cooling and sealing air flow rates)
- Mechanical efficiency η_{mec} (allows for bearing friction and wheel friction of compressor and turbine wheels)
- Heat losses through walls at turbine inlet and outlet casings $\Delta T_{GE}^*, \Delta T_{GA}^*$
- Pressure loss in intake pipe or filter-silencer at compressor inlet ΔP_{VE}^*
- Cross-sectional area at compressor outlet flange S_{VA}

B- Constructional features of engine and turbocharger system

- Number of cylinders z

- Cylinder bore d

- Piston stroke s

- Compression ratio ε

- Pre-chamber volume V_{VK} in pre-chamber diesel engines

- Maximum admissible combustion pressure $P_{\max zul}$

- Valve timings $E_{\ddot{o}}, E_S, A_{\ddot{o}}, A_S$

  - Form of inlet and outlet cross-sections as a function of the crankshaft angle $S_E = S_E(\varphi); S_A = S_A(\varphi)$ [7]   (3.3)

- Numbering of the cylinders, V-angle direction of rotation of crankshaft

- Firing sequence, firing intervals

- General layout of charging system

- Lengths and cross-sections of the individual sections of the exhaust gas ducts, including the ducts in the cylinder head

- Technical data and characteristics of any scavenging pumps, auxiliary blowers, etc.

- Technical data and characteristics of the charging air cooler $\Delta p_K^*, \varepsilon_K$ or $K.A$

C- Output data, intended use of engine

- Nominal output and nominal speed with definition (e.g. maximum continuous rating as per DIN6271, ISO standard output, etc.)

- Intended use with information on all operating points and operating curves (e.g. propeller curve) in an output diagram p_e, n specially the overload operating point and maximum torque at reduced speed
- Duration and frequency of the various operating points

D- Ambient conditions

- Atmospheric state of the environment $p_{amb}, T_{amb}, \varphi_{amb}$, minimum and maximum values, duration and frequency
- Cooling water temperature T_{kw} or cooling air temperature T_{KL} at inlet to the charging air cooler
- Pressure loss in the exhaust gas line downstream of the turbine Δp_{nT}
- Any pressure loss Δp_{vV}^* and any rise of temperature ΔT_{vV}^* of the air before entry into the compressor

E- Regulations, expectations, empirical values

- Establishing the design operating point
- Establishing the charging air state or scavenging air state
- Expected performance values, especially those of air flow, fuel consumption, and exhaust gas temperature

3.5 Turbocharger matching for two-stroke engine with constant-pressure turbo- charging system (computational)

When the calculation data as per the table have been obtained, the next step is to establish the design operating point. For this purpose the nominal output and nominal speed of the engine (P_e, n) are usually chosen in conjunction with the unfavorable atmospheric conditions $(P_{amb}, T_{amb}, \varphi_{amb})$, which can occur in the plant. [7]

The scavenging air state is then established and assumptions are made for the following operating characteristics:

- Specific air flow rate (l_e)

- Specific fuel consumption (b_e)

- Proportion of chemical energy of the fuel in the exhaust gas upstream of turbine (ζ_a)

From these assumptions, the exhaust gas temperature at the turbine inlet (T_{TE}^*) can be calculated from the equation:

$$h_{TE}^* = (h_s + \zeta_a \frac{b_e}{l_e} e_{ch}) / (1 + \frac{b_e}{l_e}) \text{ [7]} \quad (3.4)$$

With the aid of the h, T diagram for air and combustion gas *(Fig. 3.2)* and the equation number 3.4 the relationship between the specific enthalpy of the scavenging air (h_s) and of the exhaust gas at the turbine inlet (h_{TE}^*) can be shown. [7]

95

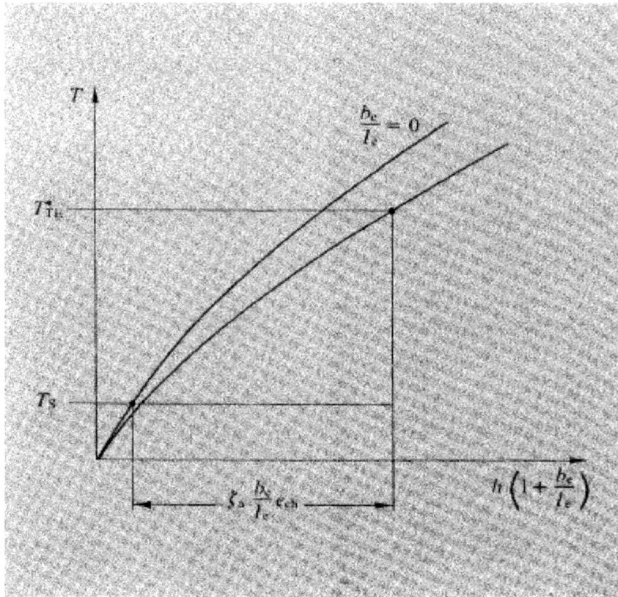

Fig. 3.2: Enthalpy-temperature diagram for air and combustion gas for
determining the exhaust gas temperature [7]

For the limited range of the usual scavenging air temperatures, a diagram can be drawn with sufficient accuracy, from which the temperature difference $T_{TE}^* - T_S$ can be read off directly *(Fig. 3.3)*. By introducing the parameter $\zeta_a \dfrac{e_{ch}}{e_{ch0}}$ in which e_{ch0} represents a fixed reference value of the chemical energy of the fuel (e.g. $e_{ch0} = 42\,MJ\,/\,kg$), the diagram can be used for all the common diesel engine fuels. The curves of Fig. 3.3 can also, be approximated by polynomials, thus enabling $T_{TE}^{*} - T_{s}$ to be simply calculated on a programmable pocket computer. [7]

However, with the aid of Fig. 3.3 the value ζ_e can easily be determined by measuring the air flow rate, the scavenging air temperature and the exhaust gas temperature.

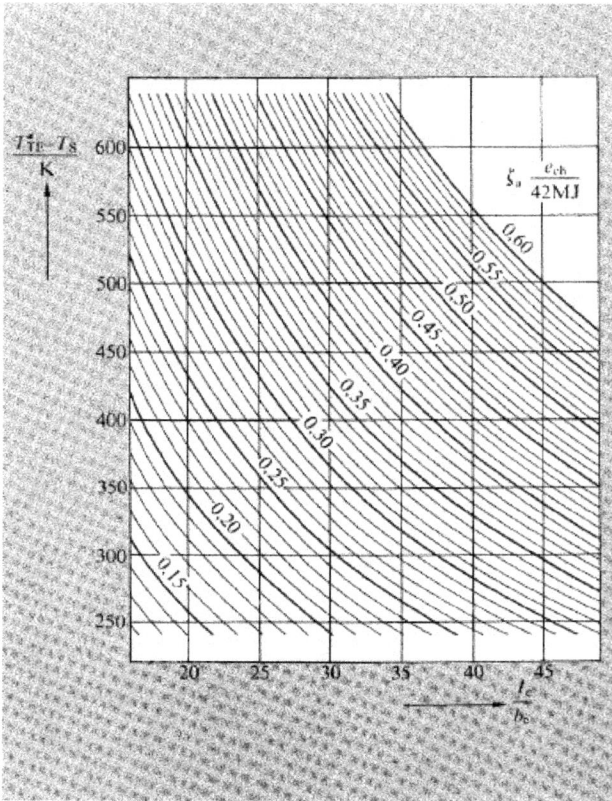

Fig. 3.3: Diagram for determining the exhaust gas temperature and the proportion of the chemical energy of the fuel in the exhaust gas [7]

If all the accessible readings are systematically collected and arranged according to the diesel engine types, turbo charging systems and other aspects, very valuable and reliable empirical curves can be obtained, as

98

shown for example in *Fig. 3.4*. If, in individual cases, insufficient values are available from experience, they can be augmented by calculated values from the working cycle. It is possible, from such working cycle calculations, to clarify in particular the influences of those parameters that are not normally varied in tests, such as the compression ratio of the engine, maximum combustion pressure, etc.

The total pressure of the exhaust gas at the turbine inlet P_{TE}^{*} is determined on the one hand by the pressure gradient necessary for scavenging the cylinders and, on the other, by the energy balance of the turbocharger. [7]

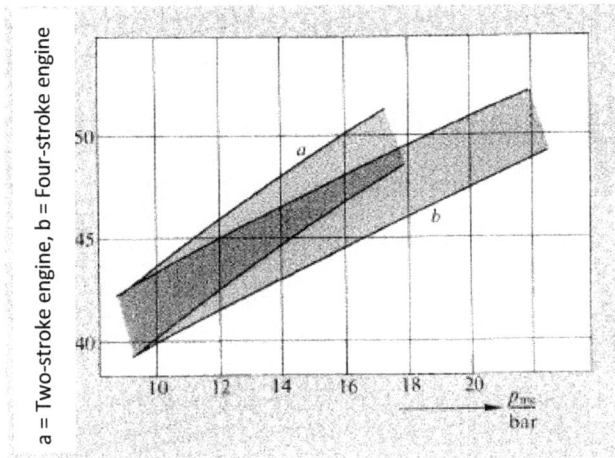

Fig. 3.4: Proportion of the chemical energy of the fuel in the exhaust gas (ζ_a) as a function of the mean effective pressure (P_{me}) [7]

The calculation of the pressure P_{TE}^* from the anticipated scavenging air flow rate In two-stroke diesel engine with constant-pressure turbocharging where the diesel engine is represented by a nozzle with isentropic flow through it, is proved to be advantageous. The cross-sectional area of this nozzle, known as the resultant scavenging cross-section of the engine $\overline{S}_{resM}$, can be calculated approximately from the graphs of the effective inlet and outlet cross-sections of the individual cylinders (Fig. 3.5).

If test results are already available from a specific engine type, its resultant scavenging cross-section can be calculated simply from the readings of scavenging air flow rate, scavenging air state and exhaust gas pressure. It is also possible in this manner to obtain empirical values of $\overline{S}_{resM}$ which are usually more accurate and reliable than those calculated from Fig. 3.5.

$$S_{resZ} = \frac{S_E x S_A}{\sqrt{S_E^2 + S_A^2}} \qquad (3.5)$$

$$S_{resM} = \frac{z}{360^0} \int_{E_O}^{A_s} S_{resZ} x d\varphi \quad (3.6)$$

100

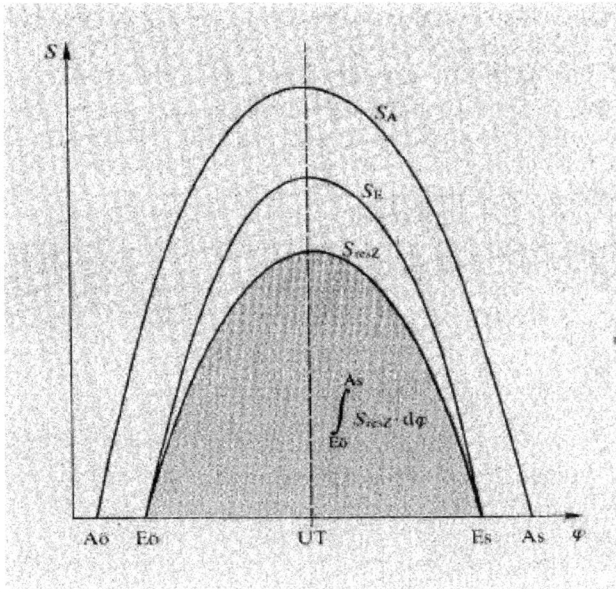

Fig.3.5: Determination of the resultant scavenging air cross-section S_{resM} of a two-stroke diesel engine [7]

After the total pressure at the turbine inlet has been calculated, it is possible, on the one hand to calculate the four turbocharger determining variables $\prod_T, S_{T_{eff}}, \prod_v^*$ and $\dot{V}_{288}$, and on the other to determine the turbocharger overall efficiency $\eta_{TL\,soll}$ required for the assumed specific air flow rate. Followings are the formulating process for determination of the turbocharger overall efficiency $\eta_{TL\,soll}$:

Expansion pressure ratio of the turbine: [7]

$$\Pi_T = \frac{P_{TE}^*}{P_{TA}} = \frac{P_{TE}^*}{P_{amb} + \Delta p_{nT}} \quad (3.7)$$

Equivalent nozzle area of the turbine: [7]

$$S_{Teff} = \frac{\dot{m}_{TE} \sqrt{R_A . T_{TE}^{*'}}}{p_{TE}^* . \Psi_m(\Pi_T, \bar{k}_A)} \quad (3.8)$$

Where:

$$T_{TE}^{*'} = T_{TE}^* - \Delta T_{GE}^* \quad (3.9)$$

$$\dot{m}_{TE} = P_e . (l_e + b_e) \quad (3.10)$$

$$\Psi_m(\Pi_T, \bar{k}_A) = \sqrt{\frac{2\bar{k}_A}{\bar{k}_A - 1}(\Pi_T^{-2/\bar{k}_A} - \Pi_T^{-(\bar{k}_A+1)/\bar{k}_A}} \quad (3.11)$$

$$(for \, \Pi_T \le \Pi_{Laval} = \left(\frac{\bar{k}_A + 1}{2}\right)^{\bar{k}_A/(\bar{k}_A - 1)}) \quad (3.12)$$

$$\Psi_m(\Pi_T, \bar{k}_A) = cons\tan t$$
$$(for \Pi_T \ge \Pi_{Laval})$$

Total pressure ratio of the compressor: [7]

$$\Pi_v^* = \frac{p_{VA}^*}{p_{VE}^*} = \frac{p_s + \Delta p_k^* + \Delta p_{dynVA}}{p_{amb} - \Delta p_{VE}^* - \Delta p_{vV}^*} \quad (3.13)$$

Note: the volumetric flow rate of the flow in the state at the compressor inlet is corrected to 15 °C (288.15 K): [7]

$$\dot{V}_{288} = \frac{\dot{m}_{VA}}{p_{VE}^*} x \sqrt{\frac{288.15}{T_{VE}^*}} = \frac{\dot{m}_{VA} . R_L \sqrt{288.15 x T_{VE}^*}}{p_{VE}^*} \quad (3.14)$$

Where:

$$\dot{m}_{VA} = l_e x P_e \quad (3.15)$$

The necessary turbocharger overall efficiency: [7]

$$\eta_{TLsoll} = \frac{\dot{m}_{VA} x \Delta h_{sV}^*}{\dot{m}_{TE} x \Delta h_{sV}^*} \quad (3.16)$$

$$\eta_{TLsoll} = \frac{1}{(1+\frac{b_e}{l_e})} x \frac{\frac{k_L}{k_L-1} R_L x T_{VE}^* (\Pi_v^{*(k_L-1)/k_L} - 1)}{\frac{\bar{k}_A}{\bar{k}_A-1} R_A x T_{TE}^* (1 - \Pi_T^{(1-\bar{k}_A)/\bar{k}_A})} \ ] \quad (3.17)$$

On the basis of the calculated determining variables for the turbocharger and by using the turbine and compressor characteristics, the appropriate specification can be selected and the actual turbocharger overall efficiency η_{TList} can be calculated. [7]

$$\eta_{TList} = \eta_{sV}^{*} x \eta_{sT}^{'} x \frac{T_{TE}^{*'}}{T_{TE}^{*}} x \eta_{vol} x \eta_{mec} \qquad (3.18)$$

If the difference between η_{TList} and η_{TLsoll} is then greater than is acceptable, the calculation should be repeated with new assumptions. As a rule, the specific air flow rate l_e is varied until the difference between η_{TList} and η_{TLsoll} is approximately equal to the difference between the efficiencies of adjacent turbocharger specifications.

Before the calculated turbocharger specification is finally established, all the calculated and assumed operating characteristic values are checked to see that they agree with the specifications, expectations and experience of the diesel engine and turbocharger manufacturers. In order to do this, certain characteristic values governing the assumptions adopted are also determined. [7]

These are, for example:

- Air flow rate λ_a and scavenging air ratio λ_s of the engine

- Volumetric efficiency λ_1 and combustion air ratio λ_s of the engine

- Final compression pressure p_c and pressure rise at combustion $p_{max} - p_c$, or the pressure ratios p_{max} / p_S that are decisive for the specific fuel consumption.

It is also necessary to check throughout the operating range of the engine that no operating characteristic variables exceed the permissible limit values throughout the whole operating range. In the turbocharger in particular, the compressor surge limit, the maximum admissible rotational speed and the maximum admissible turbine inlet temperature must be observed. If necessary the scavenging air state should be changed or a different turbocharger specification should be selected and the computation procedure then repeated. [7]

3.6 Representation of the turbine characteristics

The flow characteristic of an axial turbine with a low degree of reaction is very similar to that of an ideal nozzle with isentropic flow. A turbine of this type can therefore be very well characterized by the cross-sectional area of an equivalent nozzle of the same flow capacity. To a first approximation, the equivalent nozzle area can be calculated in the same way as the resultant cross-section of two throttles, one behind the other, in an incompressible flow, namely by: [7]

$$S_{Tres} = \frac{S_D x S_S}{\sqrt{S_D^2 + S_S^2}} \qquad (3.19)$$

Here S_D represents the narrowest cross-section of the guiding vanes, the so called nozzle area, and S_S represents the narrowest flow cross-section in the rotor blades arrangement.

The constant cross-section $S_{T\,res}$, unambiguously determined by the geometry, is well suited for the specification of different turbine variants; it is not, however, exactly equal to the equivalent nozzle area. One of the leading turbocharger manufacturers named ABB Turbo Systems Ltd, have therefore introduced the flow coefficient α_T, which is mainly dependent upon the pressure ratio Π_T, and to a slight extent also upon the tip speed ratio u/c_0. In axial- flow turbines, so following is therefore true: [7]

$S_{T\,eff} = \alpha_T(\Pi_T, u/c_0) x S_{T\,res}$ (3.20)   Where the value of α_T is rather close to unity.

For radial turbines and also certain axial-flow turbines the cross-section $S_{T\,geom}$ according to the definition of equation (3.19) is no longer even approximately equal to the equivalent nozzle cross-section $S_{T\,eff}$ Instead of $S_{T\,res}$ a different, constant reference cross-section $S_{T\,geom}$ sufficiently defined by the geometry of the turbine, has therefore been introduced so that, in general, the following applies for the equivalent nozzle area: [7]

$$S_{T\,eff} = \alpha_T(\Pi_T, u/c_0) x S_{T\,geom} \qquad (3.21)$$

The complete turbine characteristics are therefore represented by the following functions: [7]

$S_{T\,eff} = S_{T\,eff}(\Pi_T, u/c_o) = \alpha_T(\Pi_T, u/c_o) x S_{T\,geom}$

$$\eta'_{sT} = \eta'_{sT}(\Pi_T, u/c_o) \quad (3.22)$$

$$\eta_{sT} = \eta'_{sT}\frac{T^*_{TE}}{T^*_{TE}} = \eta'_{sT}\frac{T^*_{TE} - \Delta T^*_{GE}}{T^*_{TE}} \quad (3.23)$$

Allowance for the cooling ΔT^*_{GE} in the gas inlet casing is separate from the efficiency η'_{sT} of the adiabatic turbine, since either cooled or un-cooled casings can be supplied. Moreover, measurements of the turbine characteristics are frequently carried out with compressed air instead of hot gas.

In free-running turbochargers with constant-pressure admission of the turbine, the tip speed ratio u/c_o changes only within very narrow limits during steady operation. It is thus possible to represent both $S_{T\,eff}$ or α_T and η'_{sT} to a good approximation as functions of Π_T alone.

For matching calculations, the following characteristic curves are therefore used instead of an entire turbine map: [7]

$$S_{T\,eff} = S_{T\,eff}(\Pi_T) = \alpha_T(\Pi_T)xS_{T\,geom} \quad (3.24)$$

$$\eta'_{sT} = \eta'_{sT}(\Pi_T) \quad (3.25)$$

It is therefore generally unnecessary to calculate u/c_o.

3.7 A diagram for rapidly determining operating points

The computing steps of the method described here can be easily carried out by means of the aforementioned diagrams (Fig. 3.2, 3.3, 3.4) and a programmable pocket computer. Diagrams such as those described in (Fig. 3.2, 3.3, 3.4) can also be very useful for rapidly determining an approximate operating point. Their greatest use, however, is in providing an overall view of the influence of the various parameters obtained from these diagrams. An overall view can also be obtained from Fig. 3.6.

The mass flow parameter: [7]

$$\Pi_{T_{ae}} x \psi_m (\Pi_{T_{ae}}, \bar{k}_A) = \frac{\dot{m}_{TE} \sqrt{R_A x \bar{T}_{TE}^{*}}}{P_{TA} x S_{T_{ae}}} \quad (3.26)$$

Which is plotted as the abscissa?

With a constant, mean value of the isentropic exponent $\bar{k}_A$, the pressure ratio $\Pi_{T_{ae}}$ (as ordinate) can be represented by a single (broken) curve.

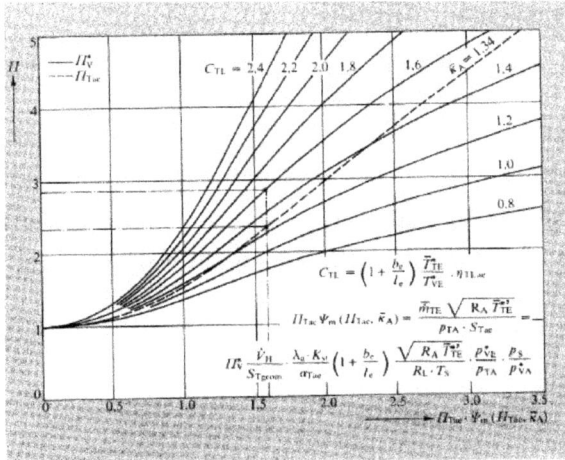

Fig. 3.6: Diagram for determining turbocharger operating points [7]

The energy balance of the turbocharger is determined by the parameter

$$C_{TL} = \frac{\bar{m}_{TE}}{\dot{m}_{VA}} x \frac{\bar{T}_{TE}^*}{T_{VE}^*}\ \eta_{TL\,ae} = (1+\frac{b_e}{l_e})\frac{\bar{T}_{TE}^*}{T_{VE}}\eta_{TL\,ae} \quad (3.27)$$

For fixed values of this parameter, it is possible, for each value of $\Pi_{T\,ae}$, to calculate the associated values of Π_V^* and also to plot them as ordinates (full curves).

For each value of the abscissa, i.e. of the mass flow parameter of equation [7]

109

$$\Pi_{T\,ae} x \psi_m (\Pi_{T\,ae}, \bar{k}_A) = \frac{\dot{m}_{TE} \sqrt{R_A x \bar{T}_{TE}^{*'}}}{P_{TA} x S_{T\,ae}} \quad (3.28)$$

$\Pi_{T\,ae}$ And Π_V^*, can therefore be directly read off. The parameter used as abscissa value should be calculated by the following formulae from the characteristic variables of the turbocharged diesel engine: [7]

$$\frac{\dot{m}_{TE} \sqrt{R_A x T_{TE}^{*'}}}{p_{TA} x S_{T\,ae}} = \Pi_V^* x \frac{\dot{V}_H}{S_{T\,geom}} x \frac{\lambda_a x K_{st}}{\alpha_{T\,ae}} (1 + \frac{b_e}{l_e}) \frac{\sqrt{R_A x T_{TE}^{*'}}}{R_L x T_S} x \frac{p_{VE}^*}{p_{TA}} x \frac{p_S}{p_{VA}^*}$$

$$(3.29)$$

The individual factors of the right side of this equation are all variables which have either to be found (e.g. $\dfrac{\dot{V}_H}{S_{T\,geom}}$ or specified, e.g. Π_v^*, p_S, T_S)

or can be estimated.

The plotted example (chain-dot line) shows how associated values of the various parameters can be read off. The diagram presented here is generally valid both for four-stroke and for two-stroke engines with a free-running turbocharger. It can be used both for constant pressure and for pulse turbo charging. The computing method set out here does not make any claim to scientific exactness, but has proved itself as a rational, flexible method in countless applications. The accuracy of the method is equivalent to the accuracy of the information on the engines and plant that is normally available. [7]

3.8 A detailed engine simulation code for matching the engine with its turbocharger and investigation of compressor surging

Surging is a vibration of audible level emanating from the compressor end of the rotating element. The compressor, depending upon its speed at any particular time, can only discharge up to a given pressure. If for any reason the pressure in the scavenge space is equal to or higher than this discharge pressure, air will attempt to flow back through the rotating impeller. In essence this is like a centrifugal pump attempting to pump against a closed valve, but with the air compressors the back flow of air throws the rotating element into a vibration, which produces the so called barking noise. [17]

There are many causes of surging. It is usually engine initiated. The turbocharger should be matched to the engine's air consumption rate and pressure across the whole operating range; this being calculated before the engine is built and tested during the shop trials. So as described in section 3.3, the transient operation of a large two-stroke marine diesel engine during compressor surging can be investigated through simulation. A detailed performance prediction code for the engine may be used in conjunction with a model capable of predicting the dynamic behavior of the turbocharger compressor. In the detailed engine simulation the steady state as well as transient simulation runs are performed and the results are validated against the experimental data which are collected during the investigation which is carried out within the context of international projects. [18]

In these projects, where the dynamics of large marine propulsion plants are investigated, an onboard Data Acquisition System (DAQ System) can be developed and installed onboard a ship. The DAQ is a shipboard, real-time computer system including the required sensors and analog-to-digital interface modules, as well as, hard disk storage capacity for the measurement data series. The DAQ System is bootstrapped around an industrial PC board with a 5x86/133 MHz processor, 4 MB DRAM, watchdog timer, 4 serial communication ports RS-232/RS-485 and 1.4 GB HDD.

Measurements can be performed during the normal trading schedule. The HDD units of the DAQ System may be designed to store the corresponding amount of data for any specified period provided that the HDD to be replaced at each port of call. A total of about 3 GB (gigabytes) of raw binary data may be recorded during the 8 months of operation of the DAQ System. This amount of data corresponds to more than 6 GB of ASCII data containing valuable information about the propulsion power plant operation under actual conditions. Part of these data can be used for the tuning and validation of the power plant simulation code as described above in this text.

Following deals in brief with a case of engine operation with turbocharger in which the problems in turbocharger matching have been extensively investigated for the design, development and optimization of the propulsion engine of a container ship. The investigation includes a simulated case of engine operation with turbocharger compressor surging.

The propulsion engine which is directly coupled to the ship propeller is a

MAN B&W 9K90MC, slow speed, two-stroke, marine diesel engine with basic characteristics as described in table 3.1. The engine is equipped with 3 ABB VTR-714 turbochargers, one air cooler connected after each turbocharger compressor for cooling the compressor discharge air, with electrically driven blowers fitted between each air cooler and the scavenging receiver for allowing adequate cylinder's air scavenging at part load engine operations.

Number of cylinders	9
Bore	900MM
Stroke	2550MM
MCR	41162Kw at 94rpm
Boost pressure at MCR	3.6bar
BMEP at MCR	18bar
Turbochargers	3 ABB VTR714

Table 3.1: The engine's basic characteristics [18]

Initially, during the investigation, steady state simulation runs at 100%, 85%, 75%, 50%, 40% and 25% loads were performed. For the simulation at 25% load, the electrically driven air blowers were considered to be activated. The required input and validation data, including the engine geometric data, the fuelling and injection timing data, the heat release rates, the compressor and turbines maps and the blower curve, were provided by the engine and turbocharger manufacturers, respectively.

A set of the derived results, including the engine brake power, the brake specific fuel consumption, the cylinder maximum pressure, the scavenging receiver pressure, the exhaust receiver temperature and the turbocharger speed, when compared with the respective parameters measured during the engine shop trials proved that the predicted results match very well the measured performance data.

After, the steady state runs, a case of engine transient operation was simulated. The engine was considered to be operating at full speed and for this case the ordered engine speed, the engine speed, the propeller shaft torque, the fuel rack position and the engine boost pressure were available. The measured ordered speed was given as input in the simulation code. In addition, the engine load torque was considered to be the measured propeller shaft torque. The governor used in the transient simulations was a standard PI governor. Due to the fact that the governor P and I constants were not known, they had to be adjusted so that the predicted fuel rack response, was in good agreement with the measured one. Thus, for various values of these constants, transient runs were performed and the simulation results compared with the experimental data. The best agreement between the experimental data and the simulation results was obtained with the values for $k_p = 0.05$ and $k_I = 0.01$.

The measured ordered engine speed and propeller load were used as input and transient runs were performed. Having validated the simulation code against steady state and transient measured data, a case of engine operation with turbocharger compressor surging was then simulated. To induce the compressor surging, the turbine of the one of the three turbochargers was considered to be dirty and the turbine swallowing capacity and efficiency were considered 10% lower than the ones of the clean turbine. The compressor of the turbocharger with the dirty turbine then exhibited surging. This was expected, because the compressor of the turbocharger with the dirty turbine is pushed by the other turbochargers to operate closer to its surge limit. Since the efficiency and the mass flow rate of the dirty turbine were reduced, the power delivery from the turbine wheel to the turbocharger shaft was lower and as a result the turbocharger speed and the compressor mass flow rate were also reduced. In addition, as the three turbochargers are connected in parallel, the compressor pressure ratio was the same for all the turbochargers. So, the compressor of the turbocharger with the dirty turbine was operating with lower speed and mass flow rate but with the same pressure ratio as the compressors of the clean turbochargers and therefore its operating point moved closer to or inside the compressor instability region. [18]

As was previously mentioned, due to the compressor surging, the scavenging receiver pressure was considerably reduced. This caused a decrease in the engine developed torque as well as the reduction of the air amount entering the engine cylinders. The former resulted in the engine speed drop since the propeller load remained almost constant, whereas the latter had as a consequence less air to be trapped inside the engine cylinders, resulting in higher gas temperatures in cylinders and exhaust gas receiver thus increasing the engine thermal loading[18]

115

From the above analysis, it can be deduced that the continuous surging of turbocharger's compressor is unacceptable for the engine operation as it leads to severe turbocharger vibrations and severe transient torsional loading to the turbocharger shaft as well as deterioration of the engine performance.

3.9 Turbocharger matching for two-stroke engine with constant-pressure turbo- charging system (in-service)

For the purpose of in-service investigation of turbocharger matching to marine slow speed two-stroke diesel engine performance, the maker of turbocharger normally supplies variants for nozzle ring and diffuser on a loan basis (matching parts).

The brief in-service matching procedures are as follow:

1. Test run of the engine with "delivery build" of the turbocharger;

2. If the charge air pressure (required by the engine manufacturer) is too low or too high, the nozzle ring must be changed (smaller nozzle for higher boost, larger nozzle for lower boost);

3. If the measured charge air pressure is accepted, the surge margin has to be checked for conformity with the manufacturer limits margin;

4. If the surge margin is below the required value, for instance 10% or less, a smaller diffuser must be used (in rare cases even a smaller compressor wheel);

5. Part load points must also be checked for adequate surge margins.

If necessary the scavenging air state should be changed or a different turbocharger specification should be selected and the computational and in-service procedures then repeated.

3.10 Conclusions

The turbocharger matching to large slow-speed marine diesel engine with its associate effects on combustion and emissions is an important issue of marine propulsion plants. So, it will be necessary for every newly specified turbocharger for a new application to be matched to optimize the turbocharger for the actual diesel engine's operation conditions and to find the most suitable build, as well as to ensure that no operating characteristic variables exceed the permissible limit values throughout the whole operating range. Therefore the following need to be determined for each engine with its turbo charging system, its output data and its ambient conditions:

- Type of turbocharger
- Size of turbocharger
- Number of turbochargers on the same engine
- Specification of the casing variants and positions, the rotor and stator blades arrangements of the compressor and turbine and variants of the bearings and lubricating system

In the turbocharger in particular, the maximum admissible rotational speed, the maximum admissible turbine inlet temperature, and the compressor surge limit must be observed. For this purpose turbochargers with a new specification are normally supplied with variants for nozzle-ring and diffuser on a loan basis (matching parts).

Therefore matching of each newly specified exhaust gas turbocharger with a large, two-stroke, marine propulsion diesel engine should have following characteristics:

- It is optimised with the best possible flow cross-sections for the operating conditions of the marine propulsion diesel engine.
- A sufficient surge-limit distance is ensured across the complete operating range. If a compressor operates near the surge line, a perturbation in the system may be enough to throw the compressor into surge. When surge occurs, the air flow reverses, and flows backward through the compressor. The flow then reverses again, and the process repeats. As one might imagine, an engine does not operate very well under this condition and disastrous effects are a serious possibility, including catastrophic failure. [19]
- Setting a limit to how fast fuel index is allowed to increase to reduce the risk of surging. One of the first steps in the series of events which may lead to surging is a significant temperature rise as experiences gained by ACME (Adaptive Control of Marine Engines) project partners indicates a correlation between the exhaust gas temperature after the turbine and the distance to the surge line on the compressor map. [20]

Engine simulation codes are widely used during the design, development and optimization of the large, marine propulsion diesel engines. Especially during the recent years, the increased complexity of such engine configuration in conjunction with the extensive usage of electronic systems for controlling the various engine parameters, introduced for improving the engine performance and reducing exhaust emissions. The utilization of detailed engine simulation codes during the engine design procedure has become progressively more commonplace in marine propulsion plant's (diesel engine) optimization process. The enhanced design of modern turbocharger's axial turbine reflects the very high efficiency and large volume flow and the design of the turbocharger's compressor reflects a wide compressor map, very high efficiency (peak efficiencies of more than 87% are obtainable), and increased volume flow.

There are numerous methods for calculating the operating characteristic variables of turbocharged marine diesel engines. They extend from simple, empirical rules for establishing variables required for turbocharger matching, to complicated, programmed procedures by which the real working cycle can be simulated in all its details. Notably since there are different turbo-charging systems of the various marine type two-stroke diesel engines, with the variable type and quantity of the information and data that the makers make available and the necessity to fulfill the diesel engine makers specifications and expectations in regard to turbocharger matching and the operating characteristic values, it is not possible to use one consistent mathematical model for calculating the operating characteristic variables of turbocharged marine diesel engines.

Full scale shipboard measurements of the propulsion plant parameters can be obtained under normal trading conditions of the ship for an extensive period. The measured data can be elaborated and several signal fragments may be used for the evaluation of the results of the simulation code.

A large part (half an hour) of the recorded propulsion plant actual transient operation can then be simulated to confirm whether the simulation results are in very good agreement with the measured data. However as per the test results on turbocharged engines, the measured data are normally in good agreement with the simulation results. This proves that the simulation code can adequately predict the dynamic response of the complete propulsion plant system. Therefore, it can be used as a tool for evaluating the results of design and operating parameters changes as well as for investigating various control options, acting as a virtual propulsion plant and thus substituting the actual experiments, which may be very costly and time-consuming.

In matching of turbocharger to marine propulsion diesel engine performance there is a complex phenomenon called compressor surging which requires special consideration as the continuous surging of turbocharger compressor may lead to the deterioration of the propulsion plant performance.

The common approach of the engine and turbocharger manufacturers towards prediction of compressor surging and its associate effects on the large slow-speed, marine diesel engine performance, is to examine the transient behavior of such diesel engine and the effect of compressor surging on engine and turbocharger operation by developing a model capable of predicting the dynamic behavior of the air compression system including compressor surging conditions. The model is then incorporated into a detailed engine simulation code. With this model, as mentioned earlier, improved results can be obtained, because the inertia of the air inside the compressor passages and the variation of the steady state compressor characteristics due to compressor transient operation are taken into consideration. Simulation of the engine operation with compressor surging is deduced by using a throttle valve after the air cooler. The result of obtained simulation data indicates that the compressor surging causes reduction in the average air flow to the cylinders, and consequently cause reduction in the air/fuel ratio, increase in exhaust gas temperature, and drop of engine torque due to the incomplete combustion. In such cases, where the obtained simulation results can contribute to better understanding of the behavior of the engine and its turbocharger in advance, appropriate control measures avoidance could be introduced for compressor surge.

3.11 List of symbols

A	Reference area for the heat transfer in the charging air cooler	n	Engine rotational speed
Aö, As	Outlet opens, outlet closes	n_{TL}	Turbocharger rotational speed
b_e	Specific fuel consumption of the engine	n_{288}	Corrected turbocharger rotational speed
c_0	$\sqrt{2\Delta h_{sT}}$	p	Absolute static speed
C_{TL}	Characteristic number for the energy balance of the turbocharger	p_{amb}	Ambient pressure
d	Cylinder bore	P_c	Final pressure of compression in cylinder
e_{ch}	Specific chemical energy of the fuel (specific calorific value, referred to the absolute temperature zero)	P_e	Useful power output of engine
e_{ch0}	Reference value of e_{ch}	P_{max}	Maximum firing pressure

Eö, Es	Inlet opens, inlet closes	$P_{max\ zul}$	Permissible max. firing pressure
h	Specific enthalpy	P_{me}	Break mean effective pressure(BMEP) of the engine
h_s	Specific enthalpy of the scavenging air and charging air in the inlet manifold.	P_{TA}	Static pressure at the turbine outlet
h_{TE}^*	Specific total enthalpy of the exhaust gas at the turbine inlet		
$\bar{h}_{TE}^\cdot$	Mean energy value of $h_{TE}^\cdot$ for pulsating turbine admission	$P_{\dot{T}E}$	Pressure at turbine inlet under total conditions
$\Delta h_s T$	Specific, isentropic enthalpy head of the turbine	$P_{\dot{T}Eae}$	Value of $P_{\dot{T}E}$ for equivalent constant pressure turbine admission
S_{Tgeom}	Reference cross-sectional area defined by the turbine geometry	$P_{\dot{V}A}$	Pressure at compressor outlet under total conditions
S_{Tres}	Resultant flow area of axial turbines	$P_{\dot{V}E}$	Pressure at compressor inlet under total conditions (downstream of

			suction branches of filter silencer)
S_{VA}	Cross-sectional area at the compressor outlet flange	ΔP_{dynVA}	Lost proportion of the dynamic pressure at the compressor outlet
T	Absolute static temperature	$\Delta P_{\dot{K}}$	Pressure drop in charging air cooler under total conditions
T_{amb}	Ambient temperature	ΔP_{nT}	Pressure drop in the gas line downstream of the turbine
T_{KW}, T_{KL}	Cooling water and cooling air temperature upstream of the charging air cooler	$\Delta P_{\dot{V}E}$	Pressure drop in the suction branches or filter silencer at the compressor inlet under total conditions
T_s	Scavenging air and charging air temperature	$\Delta P_{\dot{V}V}$	Pressure drop in the air duct upstream of the compressor (when provided)
T_{TA}^*	Temperature at turbine outlet under total conditions	R_l	Gas constant of the air
T_{TE}^*	Temperature at turbine inlet under total conditions	R_A	Gas constant of the exhaust gas
$T_{\dot{T}\dot{E}}$	$T_{TE}^* - \Delta T_{GE}^*$	s	Piston stroke

$T^*_{T\dot{E}}$	Mean energy value of $T^*_{T\dot{E}}$ for pulsating turbine admission	S	Cross-sectional area
$T^*_{V\dot{E}}$	Temperature at the compressor inlet	S_A	Isentropic flow area of the outlet valves or ports
ΔT^*_{GE}	Drop in exhaust gas temperature in the gas inlet casing of the turbine	S_D	Cross-sectional area of the turbine nozzle ring
ΔT^*_{vV}	Increase in the air temperature upstream of the compressor	S_E	Isentropic flow area of the inlet valves or ports
u	Tip speed of turbine rotor	S_{resM}	Resultant scavenging flow area of the engine (mean valve)
UT	Lower dead centre of piston	$\bar{S}_{resZ}$	Resultant scavenging flow area of one cylinder (instantaneous valve)
V_h	Swept volume of one cylinder	S_S	Minimum flow area of the rotor blading
$\dot{V}_H$	Swept volume of the entire engine per unit of time	S_{Tae}	Equivalent nozzle area for equivalent constant-pressure turbine admission

V_{VK}	Pre-chamber volume for pre-chamber diesel engine	S_{Teff}	Equivalent turbine nozzle area
$\dot{V}_{288}$	Volume flow of delivery rate under compressor inlet conditions, corrected to 15 C(288-15K)	η'_{sTae}	Isentropic turbine efficiency without heat through the wall for equivalent constant-pressure admission
z	Number of cylinders of the engine	η^*_{sV}	Isentropic compressor efficiency (total conditions at the inlet and outlet)
α_T	Flow coefficient of the turbine	η_{TL}	Overall efficiency of the turbocharger
α_{Tae}	Flow coefficient for equivalent constant pressure turbine admission	$\eta_{TLsoll}, \eta_{TList}$	Required and actual overall efficiency of turbocharger
Δ	Difference	η_{TLae}	Overall efficiency of the turbocharger for equivalent constant-pressure turbine admission
ε	Compression ratio of the engine (as per DIN 1940)	η_{vol}	Volumetric efficiency of the compressor
ε_k	Thermal ratio of the charging air cooler	k_L	Isentropic exponent of the air

ξ_a	Proportion of chemical energy of the fuel in the exhaust gas at the turbine inlet	$\bar{k}_A$	Mean isentropic exponent of the exhaust gas
η_{mec}	Mechanical efficiency of the turbocharger	λ_A	Air flow of the engine
$\mu_s T$	Isentropic turbine efficiency (total conditions at the inlet/static pressure at the outlets)	λ_l	Volumetric efficiency of the engine
$\eta_s' T$	Isentropic turbine efficiency without heat through the wall	λ_s	Scavenging air ratio of engine
		λ_v	Combustion air ratio of the engine
Δh_{sV}^*	Specific, isentropic delivery head of the compressor	Π_{Laval}	Expansion pressure ratio for which an isentropic flow attains the speed of sound
Δh_{sTae}	Specific, isentropic enthalpy head of the turbine for equivalent constant pressure turbine admission	Π_T	Expansion pressure ratio of the turbine(pressure under total conditions at the inlet and under static conditions at the outlet)

k	Heat transfer coefficient of the charging air cooler with the reference area A	Π_{Tae}	Expansion pressure ratio for equivalent constant-pressure turbine admission
K_{St}	'Pulse factor', correction factor for the equivalent nozzle area of the turbine	Π^*_V	Pressure ratio of the compressor (pressure under total conditions at inlet and outlet)
l_e	Specific air flow of the engine	ρ_s	Density of the scavenging and charging air in the inlet manifold
$\dot{m}_{TE}$	Exhaust gas mass flow at the turbine inlet	ρ^*_{vE}	Density of the air under total conditions at the compressor inlet
$\overline{\dot{m}}_{TE}$	Mean value of $\dot{m}_{TE}$	φ	Crank angle
$\dot{m}_{VA}$	Air mass flow at the compressor outlet	φ_{amb}	Relative humidity of the ambient air
ψ_m	Function for calculating the isentropic mass flow through a nozzle		

Glossary

ABB	A leading turbo charger manufacturer located in Baden, Switzerland
Abscissa	The horizontal coordinate of a point in a plane Cartesian coordinate system obtained by measuring parallel to the x-axis
Adiabatic	Occurring without loss or gain of heat
Ambiguously	Doubtful or uncertain especially from obscurity or indistinctness
Analogy	A comparison of one thing with another thing that has similar features
ASCII	American Standard Code for Information Interchange, ASCII is a code for representing English characters as numbers, with each letter assigned a number from 0 to 127
Attenuation	To make thin or slender
Bootstrapped	To promote or develop by initiative and effort with little or no assistance
Cat-fines	Catalyst fines, abrasive particulates in bunker fuel
Co2	Carbon dioxide

Compensator	To make an appropriate and usually counterbalancing payment to
Compensator	To be equivalent to: counterbalance
Comprehended of	To grasp the nature, significance, or meaning
Containment	The act, process, or means of containing
Converged another	To tend or move toward one point or one
Criterion may be based	A standard on which a judgment or decision
Deterioration	The action or process of deteriorating
Diffuser	A device (as a reflector) for distributing the light of a lamp evenly
Diffusion	The process whereby particles of liquids, gases, or solids intermingle as the result of their spontaneous movement caused by thermal agitation and in dissolved substances move from a region of higher to one of lower concentration
DRAM	Dynamic Random Access Memory, a type of memory used in most personal computers
Endothermic	Characterized by or formed with absorption of

heat

Enhance	To increase or improve in value, quality, desirability, or attractiveness
Equation	A usually formal statement of the equality or equivalence of mathematical or logical expressions
Equilibrium	A state of intellectual or emotional balance
Excitation	The disturbed or altered condition resulting from stimulation of an individual, organ, tissue, or cell
Exothermic heat	Characterized by or formed with expulsion of
Exponent	A symbol written above and to the right of a mathematical expression to indicate the operation of rising to a power
Fixed-Pitch	Referred to propellers with fixed blades
Granulates	To form or crystallize into grains or granules
HDD	Hard Disk Drive, the mechanism that reads and writes data on a hard disk
Hitherto	Up to this or that time
IMO	International Maritime Organization

Impede	To interfere with or slow the progress of
Impeller	Blade of a rotor
Imply	To contain potentially
Intermittently	Coming and going at intervals
Isentropic	Of or relating to equal or constant entropy
Labyrinth	A place constructed of or full of intricate passageways and blind alleys
Multi-Lobe	Multi processor
NOx	Nitrogen oxide
Preceding	To surpass in rank, dignity, or importance
Predominant authority	Having superior strength, influence, or
Propeller	A device that consists of a central hub with radiating blades placed and twisted so that each forms part of a helical surface and that is used to propel a vehicle
Propulsion	The action or process of propelling
Scavenging	To remove (as dirt or refuse) from an area
Silencer	The muffler of an internal combustion engine
Simulation	To give or assume the appearance or effect of

often with the intent to deceive

Skepticism	An attitude of doubt or a disposition to incredulity either in general or toward a particular object
Spatial	Relating to, occupying, or having the character of space
Surge	To rise and fall actively
Swallowing	To take through the mouth and esophagus into the stomach
Thermodynamic	Being or relating to a system of atoms, molecules, colloidal particles, or larger bodies considered as an isolated group in the study of thermodynamic processes
Volute	A spiral or scroll-shaped form

References

1- MAN B&W Turbochargers, Electronic support system, (2004) and MAN B&W Diesel AG, TCA Turbocharger, Project Guide, (June 2003), D 2366240e

2- Somer, A, Jack and Brown, David, (1998) The Sulzer Diesel Engine, ISBN 3-9521561-0-8, Vol.1

3- Dunn, D. (2001) Fundamental Engineering Thermodynamics, Pearson Education Limited, ISBN 0-582-43217-0

4- Klein Woud, J. and Stapersma, D. (2002) Design of propulsion and electric power generation system, IMarEST, ISBN 1-902536-47-9

5- Publication number CH-Z 3043 99 E, (1999) and Electronic performance support system, Version 1.6 (December 2001) ABB turbo system Ltd., Baden, Switzerland

6- Schieman, J. (1995) Turbocharger compressors, Turbo magazine, Issue no. I, Vol.1

7- Meire, E. A simple method of calculation for matching turbochargers, ABB Turbo Systems Ltd. Internal Paper, Revision 5-81, Baden, Switzerland

8- Schieman, J. (1995) Turbocharger turbines, Turbo magazine, Issue no. II, Vol.1

9- Watson,D. G. (1998) Practical ship design, Elsevier ocean engineering series, Vol.1, ISBN 0-08-042999-8

10- Tinsley, D. (2004) Noise and vibration, IMAREST publication, Marine Engineers Review, April 2004

11- Clay, D. C. and Moch, S. W. (2002) Development of a new test facility for evaluation of turbocharger noise emissions, IMechE Conference Transaction, ISBN 1-86058-383-0, Vol.1

12- Joel, R. (1996) Basic Engineering Thermodynamics, Pearson Education Ltd. Fifth edition, ISBN 0-582-25629-1

13- Reference number ISO 8217: 1996(E), International standard, Petroleum products, Fuels (class F), Specifications of marine fuels, Second edition

14- Freeman, P. F. and Walsham, B. E. (1978), a guide to some analytical matching techniques, paper No. C 59/78, The Institution of Mechanical Engineers, Conference about Turbocharging and turbochargers, London 1978

15- Kumamoto, H. and Henley, E. J. (1996), Probabilistic risk assessment and management for engineers and scientists, Second edition, ISBN 0-7803-1004-7

16- Woods, Robert, L. (1997) Modeling and simulation of dynamic systems, Prentice-Hall, Inc. ISBN 0-13-337379-1

17- Cowly, J. (1992) The running and maintenance of marine machinery, Institute of marine engineer, Sixth edition, ISBN 0-907206-42-5

18- Theotokatos, G. and Kyrtatos, N. P. (2002) Analysis of a large two-stroke diesel engine transient behavior during compressor surging, IMechE Conference Transaction, ISBN 1-86058-383-0, Vol.1

19- Chapman, K. S. and Brentano, T. L. and Malicke, D. (2001) Design and construction of a large bore engine flow bench to experimentally determine port discharge coefficient for better prediction of air flow, ASME fall technical conference proceedings, Argonne national laboratory, Argonne, September 23-26, 2001

20- Bulaty, T. and Skopil, M. and Codan, E. (1994) A flexible simulation system for turbocharged diesel engine, ABB Technique 6/7/1994, S.30-37.

Intentionally Blank

نوبت چاپ:	اول - ۱۳۹۶	
تیراژ:	۱۰۰۰ نسخه	
ویراستار:	مروارید عابدیان کاسگری	

سرشناسه:	**کشاورزی، حمید، ۱۳۳۶ –**
	Kheshavarzi, Hamid
عنوان و نام پدیدآور:	Selection and Matching Turbocharger to Large Propulsion Engine Performance / Hamid Keshavarzi; edited by Morvarid, Abedian Kasgari.
مشخصات نشر:	تهران: نشر دگراندیشان، ۱۳۹۶= ۲۰۱۷م.
مشخصات ظاهری:	۱۴۰ ص. : مصور (رنگی)، جدول، نمودار.
شابک:	۹۷۸-۶۰۰-۹۷۷۷۳-۶-۵
وضعیت فهرست‌نویسی:	فیپا
یادداشت:	انگلیسی.
یادداشت:	کتابنامه.
آوانویسی عنوان:	سلکشن ...
موضوع:	موتورهای دیزل -- دستگاه‌های سوخت
موضوع:	Diesel motor -- Fuel systems
موضوع:	موتورهای درونسوز -- دستگاه‌های سوخت
موضوع:	Internal combustion engines -- Fuel systems
موضوع:	توربوشارژرها
موضوع:	Turbochargers
شناسه افزوده:	عابدیان کاسگری، مروارید، ۱۳۷۶ –
شناسه افزوده:	Abedian Kasgari, Morvarid
رده‌بندی کنگره:	TJ ۷۹۵/۵ک۸س ۱۳۹۶
رده‌بندی دیویی:	۶۲۱/۴۳۶
شماره کتابشناسی ملی:	۴۹۰۱۶۵۵

telegram.me/degarandishanpublication

instagram.com/degarandishanpublication

twitter.com/degarandishanpublication

www.degarandishan.com

ناشر: موسسه انتشارات دگراندیشان

تهران: صندوق پستی ۱۹۵۷۵/۵۷۱

Selection

and

Matching

Turbocharger

to

Large

Propulsion

Engine

Performance

موسسه انتشارات دگراندیشان

www.ingramcontent.com/pod-product-compliance
Lightning Source LLC
Chambersburg PA
CBHW071133280326
41935CB00010B/1205